W9-BWN-115

JOAN MURRAY (1917–1942) was born during an air raid in London. She was the daughter of Stanley Webster Murray, a painter and illustrator, and Florence Margaret Murray, a diseuse. She spent her early years in London, Paris, and Ontario, and lived most of her short life in the United States, where she studied dance and theater, and poetry with W. H. Auden at the New School. She suffered from rheumatic fever as a child, the complications of which led to a chronic heart condition and eventually to her death.

FARNOOSH FATHI is the author of the poetry collection *Great Guns* and founder of the Young Artists Language & Devotion Alliance (YALDA). She lives and teaches in New York, most recently at Stanford Online High School, Poets House, The Poetry Project, and Columbia University.

JOHN ASHBERY (1927–2017) was the author of several books of poetry, including *Self-Portrait in a Convex Mirror* (1975), which received the Pulitzer Prize for Poetry, the National Book Critics Circle Award, and the National Book Award. His first collection, *Some Trees* (1956), was selected by W. H. Auden for the Yale Series of Younger Poets. From 1990 until 2008 he was the Charles P. Stevenson Jr. Professor of Languages and Literature at Bard College.

In this Hour We Will Sleep.

The autemn flairs itself like a drum of colour.
Cool are your arms about my kneck and we cling.
Deep is the beat of hearts,softly the brush of
leaves
Slipping over us,molding us to the autemn earth.

In this hour we will sleep,
Mouth to mouth,twinned and deep.
~~Brush leaves rustle~~...~~fall~~ O my love
~~Drop~~: very:all our sleep
~~Sleep~~ O keep us to our this sleep

And quiet leaves include
hide us in to
this to~ / they ever
sl our sleep in all this leaf

While

The sun is a thin burnt line of red.
It is the time when life curls and broods,
When my tired,lean summer hands shake with desire
Drawing you warm to ~~my~~ *feet* stored harvest ~~fller from~~ an
autemn ~~earth~~..*a hand*
good talk us
In this hour we will sleep,
Mouth to mouth,twinned and deep.
~~Dry leaves rustle~~....*fall*
Drop....
~~Sleep~~

autumn lover
and my dream lover

split
split

Quiet leaves keep to us key

Joan Murray

Drafts, Fragments, and Poems
The Complete Poetry

EDITED AND WITH AN INTRODUCTION
BY FARNOOSH FATHI
PREFACE BY JOHN ASHBERY

NYRB/POETS

 NEW YORK REVIEW BOOKS   New York

THIS IS A NEW YORK REVIEW BOOK
PUBLISHED BY THE NEW YORK REVIEW OF BOOKS
435 Hudson Street, New York, NY 10014
www.nyrb.com

Library of Congress Cataloging-in-Publication Data
Names: Murray, Joan, 1917–1942, author. | Ashbery, John, 1927–2017, writer
  of preface. | Fathi, Farnoosh, 1981– editor.
Title: Drafts, fragments, and poems : the complete poetry / Joan Murray;
  preface by John Ashbery; edited by Farnoosh Fathi.
Description: New York: New York Review Books, 2018. | Series: New York
  Review Books Poets
Identifiers: LCCN 2017044457 (print) | LCCN 2017052741 (ebook) | ISBN
  9781681371832 (epub) | ISBN 9781681371825 (softcover)
Subjects: | BISAC: POETRY / American / General.
Classification: LCC PR6025.U743 (ebook) | LCC PR6025.U743 A6 2018
  (print) | DDC 821/.912—dc23
LC record available at https://lccn.loc.gov/2017044457

ISBN 978-1-68137-182-5
Available as an electronic book; ISBN 978-1-68137-183-2

Cover and book design by Emily Singer

Printed in the United States of America on acid-free paper.
10 9 8 7 6 5 4 3 2 1

Contents

LETTERS AND PROSE

DRAFTS, FRAGMENTS, AND POEMS

APPENDIX

PREFACE

[Originally published in the Poetry Project Newsletter *(October/ November 2003) and in John Ashbery's* Selected Prose *(University of Michigan Press, 2005)—here revised and expanded.]*

ONE OF THE POETS of the forties whom I most enjoy re-reading is Joan Murray, author of the 1947 volume *Poems by Joan Murray* in the Yale Series of Younger Poets. (She is not to be confused with the contemporary poet Joan Murray, author of *Queen of the Mist, Looking for the Parade,* and *The Same Water.*) Very little is known of her life, and what little biographical information I have comes from George Bradley, who did research on her when compiling *The Yale Younger Poets Anthology* (Yale, 1988). I haven't had a chance to consult her archives, which are at the Smith College Library.

Murray was born February 12, 1917, in London, apparently of Canadian parents who had met in Toronto. Her father, Stanley, was a painter. Her mother, Margaret or Peggy, had aspirations to become an actress and advertised herself as a diseuse or monologist, a genre whose most famous exponent was the American Ruth Draper. The couple soon separated and by 1927 Peggy and young Joan were back in North America, living in Chatham, Ontario, and Detroit (where Peggy had a sister), and eventually in New York. Joan's health was always frail; she had rheumatic fever in 1930 and thereafter, and eventually died of a heart valve infection on January 4, 1942, a month before her twenty-fifth birthday, in Saranac Lake, NY.

In New York Joan studied dance and acting, the latter at the School of Dramatic Arts under the famous Russian actress Maria Ouspenskaya. In the fall of 1940 she studied poetry with W. H. Auden at the New School. They became friends and Auden chose her posthumous volume as the first during his tenure as judge of the Yale Series of Younger Poets, which lasted from 1947 to 1959. (Her finest poetry was all written in the scant year and a half between meeting Auden and her tragic early death; Bradley says "the great outpouring of high-quality work all happened within a year.") The book was edited by a little-known poet named Grant Code, a friend of Peggy's who hadn't known Joan. He admitted that he did so with a rather free hand, but we have only his versions of most of the poems; a box containing the original manuscripts was lost by moving men when the archives were shipped to Smith College some time in the 1960s.*

Although it seems unlikely that Code could have improved on the originals, we are lucky to have his versions;

---

* Editor's note: This box, of course, was later found. See the editor's introduction to this volume.

my impression is that Murray's poetry was powerful enough to stand up to the ministrations of a well-meaning but somewhat heavy-handed editor. The volume seems not to have attracted much attention when it was published. Bradley, who calls it "one of the high points in the series," says that reviewers were "puzzled." William Meredith, however, gave it a mostly laudatory review in *Poetry* (September, 1947), saying that the book "introduces a powerful and distinctive voice. The distinction is not achieved without sacrifices, often of clarity, sometimes of music, but all the cost is justified by the fresh excellence of the best of Joan Murray's poems. These make strong reading."

Grant Code said that she left most of her poems untitled, and that he therefore chose the first line of a poem as its title in many instances, using her title if there was one, and occasionally supplying one of his own. Using the first line turns out to have been a good idea; just reading the table of contents gives one an idea of the strength and sharpness of her work. Here are a few titles: "If, here in the city, lights glare from various source," "There are shapes out of the North," "The Young Host of Rockledge," "Poem: For Dai," "You Spoke of Windmills," "Not that I had ever laughed too much," "Talk of People in Warning," "Here where I tamper at the inverted walls of tomorrow," "I feel only the desolation of wide water," and "Even the gulls of the cool Atlantic retip the silver foam."

These I think demonstrate her power of abruptly inducting the reader into the poem in media res. In fact the second, third, and succeeding lines often veer in quite other directions. In "Here where I tamper..." we scarcely get a chance to wonder about the nature of "the inverted walls of tomorrow" or what "tampering" with them could involve; the poem is already off and running. The second stanza is typical of her whirlwind trajectories.

Leave the head to its particular swimming
The hand as fist where it belongs, the finger to its
    skimming.
Know the new, and meet again the adult
Walk the path with men and women and consult
The attitudes of little children.
Treat with gravity the statement of the parrot and
    the hen;
Run with your hands in pockets whistling and listen
    to sharp wisdom
From your own spontaneous play, even from
The clip of your heels under night lamps and on in
    the dark;
While hieroglyph trees are marked thin and bare
    about the winter park.

Here we have her fondness for unexpected rhymes (children/hen; wisdom/from), perhaps as a result of Auden's influence, and for lines of unequal length, suggestive of waves washing up on a beach, with every so often an unusually long one, like the wave that surprises you when you're walking by the ocean, making you run to escape it. (The sea is often a backdrop for her poems, though knowing little about her life I am not aware if she ever lived near a seacoast.) What is most startling here and elsewhere in her work are the abrupt transitions and changes of scene: the head and its particular swimming, the finger skimming, the attitudes of little children, the statements of parrot and hen, running with hands in pockets, the clip of heels under night lamps in the winter park. How did we get from there to here, and what have we been told? As so often, this remains partly or largely mysterious. What we are left with is the sense of an act accomplished, an act of telling, and a feeling we must take this communication away to study it; something important is hidden there. Repeated readings may not reveal it, but the mere act of reading Murray's poetry always seems to be pushing one closer to the brink of a momentous discovery.

Since Joan Murray is almost by definition a poet of incompleteness, of "uncollectedness," it's fitting that we now have a new presentation of her Yale Series of Younger Poets manuscript, together with the satellite poems that originally accompanied it. The meanings of her poems are embedded somewhere in the fluidity and irregularity of her language.

By choosing to include Murray's fragments, letters, a newly discovered verse play ("The Dream of the Architect"), and by returning her poems to what we can assume is close to their intended form, poet Farnoosh Fathi has performed a valuable service of retrieval that will bolster the reputation of this most overlooked of poets. It's as if the texts are given new space to breathe.

—*John Ashbery*

INTRODUCTION

JOAN MURRAY'S untimely death from a congenital heart condition in 1942, at age twenty-four, marked the loss of an extraordinary poet. The tragic facts only heighten the epic achievement of her work. Like Emily Dickinson and Laura Riding, Murray belongs to a radical arc of American metaphysical women poets, most of whom remain unsung and who evince, as Murray wrote in a letter to her mother, "What truth, what mystical awareness can be lived." Like the young Rimbaud, Murray intended to make herself a seer—what she calls, among other figures, the "Unemployed or universal Architect." She achieved this not, as Rimbaud proposed, by a total derangement of the senses but by building "the firm reality of a consciousness, consciousness in the never-ending, the great wideness that one must blend withal." Murray's poems recalibrate the notion of a life's work and testify to the rigor and brilliance with which she realized her vision.

Five years after her death, out of the blue in 1947, her first book of poetry was published as the winner of the Yale

Series of Younger Poets Competition with the title *Poems by Joan Murray: 1917–1942*. W.H. Auden, who had been dissatisfied with the manuscripts he had received as a first-year judge, had reached out to Murray's mother to inquire about the possibility of publishing her daughter's work posthumously for the prize. Murray had been a student in Auden's Poetry and Culture course at the New School in 1940, and her mother countered Auden's invitation with the accusation that he had killed her daughter by inspiring her "poetry fever." But she was devoted to her daughter's work and eager to see it published, so agreed to the Yale edition with the condition that her friend Grant Code—a poet, Harvard lecturer, and dance and theater critic—edit the collection.

While Murray's *Poems* received mostly laudatory reviews in *Poetry*, the *Saturday Review*, *The New York Times Book Review*, and *The New Yorker*, it soon fell into obscurity and remained out of print for more than fifty years. I first learned about the collection in 2006, thanks to the poet Shanna Compton who posted an invaluable pdf of it on the PhillySound blog's "Neglectorino Project," a series on neglected writers started by the poet CAConrad. In a note to the pdf, Compton writes, "Despite the untimely death of the author, the flawed editorial work, and the fact that the book has been out of print for decades, Murray has managed to earn something of an underground reputation." How was it possible that Murray's poems—with their wild and unwavering authority, their singular metaphysics of a migratory American psyche, one unburdened by any formal or aesthetic "schooling" and the clearest evidence we've ever had of the visionary nature of youth, what George Eliot averred of the young Teresa of Ávila whose "passionate nature demanded an epic life" and who found her epos in poetry—how could these poems be so totally unknown? And so the seeds for *Drafts, Fragments, and Poems* were planted.

Joan Margaret Murray was born in London on February 12, 1917, during an air raid. She was born to Canadian parents, Stanley Webster Murray and Florence "Peggy" Margaret Murray (née Poaps)—parents who affectionately called her "Twinks." Stanley, the son of a well-known Presbyterian minister in Toronto, had served in the war with a British infantry regiment and later became a successful portraitist and illustrator. Peggy worked as a traveling diseuse, a monologist who could also sing and dance. At some point Murray decided she preferred the middle name "Vincent"—from the Latin *vincere*, "to conquer"—and often signed her poems Joan Vincent Murray.

The family moved frequently—to London, Paris, and Ontario—until Stanley and Peggy separated in the early 1920s, when Murray was about seven. At age ten, she was sent to live with the Jacksons, her maternal aunt and uncle, and their three children, in Chatham, Ontario, where she spent the rest of her childhood. Despite long stretches without seeing her mother, Murray maintained an intimate bond with her, the two corresponding extensively throughout Murray's life, sometimes on a daily basis. Her father, though, dropped out of her life and seldom kept in contact.

Murray suffered her first bout of rheumatic fever when she was eleven, leaving her with a permanently damaged heart valve and susceptibility to recurring infections. Her condition required constant vigilance and extensive rest, but Murray was restless. Two years later, at age thirteen, she suffered an even more acute attack, one so severe that death seemed certain according to her doctors. But she survived it.

Murray's formal schooling was irregular and incomplete. In the fall of 1929, she and her cousins Jean and Betty Jackson were sent to a local Ursuline convent boarding school, the Pines, which she attended off and on until 1932. That August, at the age of fifteen, she immigrated to Detroit, Michigan, with the Jacksons. In her passport photo she wears a serious, fiercely radiant expression, a blazer and tie, and a slick curtain crew cut. In Detroit, she finished the ninth grade at the Miss Newman School, but her secondary schooling ended there. A letter from Headmistress Newman described her as wholly unsuited to a conventional education, possessing an exceptionally sophisticated sensibility—"lovely, modest" and "a soul apart."

From then on Murray directed her own studies, focusing on writing, acting, and dance. She often worried about gaps in her education and struggled resolutely to fill them through a rigorous daily schedule and ambitious reading lists that reveal the breadth and depth of her study, as noted in this letter to her mother, which she wrote when she was seventeen:

> I was lying in bed yesterday thinking I ought to be creating something or other, that awful nagging feeling a writer gets, you know when suddenly the idea

came that I should write nine dedicatory poems to the great people that I feel I know so intimately, the first five to those who are dead: Duncan, Terry, Bernhardt, Duse and Irving; the other four to Bori, Lily Pons, Barrymore and Le Gallienne—some job, what? The first on Le Gallienne probably breaks all the rules of poetry, grammar, punctuation, etc.

Even as a teenager, Murray always kept several dedicated irons in the fire and held high ambitions for her creative endeavors. A notable 1934 side project, "The Hills and the Hollows," her childhood memoir in blank verse, describes a vision she had at age three of a ring of "two-inch miners" that she tried to save from a "lizard-sized dragon." "It was a vision that a labor-union or communist St. Joan might have had," she reflected, suggesting the kind of person and writer she aspired to become. Yet Murray's primary desire at seventeen was to write for the theater and act. She was at work on her first major play, *The Son of Pan*, with hopes of the writer-director-actress Eva Le Gallienne, a pioneer of the American repertory movement, producing it. She writes to her mother:

I care too much about the theatre to wish to clutter it up with any more superfluous drama. Give me a year and I'll give you a play! I'll write it all over again. I'll make it live! Put some strength into it! My main character is too interesting to handle in the manner I have. I should go more deeply into all the characters, make the poetry more unified and carry the play on to an ending truly worthy of the Son of Pan. Whether I can do this or not I don't know. All I know is that I feel much happier at the thought. I mean business!

Murray's dream to study theater at the prestigious Irvine School compelled her to move to New York when she turned eighteen. She acted and danced semiprofessionally, first with Theodora Irvine and the Irvine Players, continuing later to study theater with Tamara Daykarhanova and Maria Ouspenskaya and to dance with Mikhail Mordkin.

When she was twenty she met the novelist Helen Anderson, and though they only saw each other in person four times, theirs was a marriage of true minds, the kind Murray shared with few others, and they corresponded frequently with a devotional intensity. The friendship with Anderson played a significant part in Murray's decision to focus on writing and less on acting. At her friend's suggestion, Murray started writing a novel but became so frustrated with it, she made little progress. She dreamed of joining Anderson and her boyfriend in an artist commune in Oregon and of becoming an ascetic "in a turret or in a desert with a sack cloth and nothing more." But her mother insisted that Murray's health prohibited such a move.

By the fall of 1937, Murray felt even more caged by the theater and city life, and continued to plot a move to the northwest or to her native England. She headed back to Detroit without plans and stayed for two years, ever hungry for "crits" on her stunted novel and for artistic community. She studied part-time at the University of Michigan, where one course in Far Eastern art deepened her interest in Buddhist thought. And then in a short-story writing workshop with Donald Hamilton Haines in the fall of 1938, she found the guidance she craved. Haines encouraged her as a writer and advised her to delay publishing, advice she heeded. But a critical poetic revelation was imminent.

Murray had read and written poems since she was a child—A. E. Housman's *A Shropshire Lad* was one of her favorites—but reading Yeats when she was twenty-two spurred a conversion. Her transformation was sealed by the spring of 1940 when she moved back to New York and enrolled in W. H. Auden's Poetry and Culture class at the New School, and then continued her studies with him in the fall in his seminar "The Language and Technique of Poetry." Auden was already a renowned poet at age thirty-three, and Murray found in him a kindred spirit, as she wrote to her mother: "I may ask Auden for crits because our struggles are in many ways alike and we are more of an age. As a creative artist he has not only talked but led. He has used his knowledge." In the summer of 1940, between semesters, Murray and Auden exchanged many letters and their friendship grew. She worked and reworked her letters to him many times, characteristically using correspondence to formulate her own poetics and thoughts about art. She also continued to send him poems to read. In April 1941, Auden chose Murray's poem "Orpheus: Three Eclogues" for publication in the magazine *Decision: A Review of Free Culture*, the first and only poem published in her lifetime.

The last three years of Murray's life were her happiest, and marked by intense creative productivity, as she wrote to a friend in 1941:

There is the fresh imagination and understanding. I may hit directly to the core of the intellectual intuitive. One almost has to forget that others have thought before one so that the essentials may be alive and not inhibited by the second- or third-hand reaction generally exhaled. The mind of an Unemployed or universal Architect epitomized in the desire to recreate what is desolated, to rebuild; the fact that the spirit exists beside every terrible destruction; that the sensitive but inarticulate line is being put upon innumerable plans while all is in shambles. The characters are of course symbolic. The jungle that the whole thing may or may not pull through is pretty nerve-wracking. But as I have mentioned, I ask myself the question and the rest is inordinate adventure.

She undertook extensive, solitary walking trips in the northeast, hiking the hills and valleys of Vermont and Massachusetts, often fifteen miles a day, from town to town, stopping to read and to write letters to her mother, and cavorting with other artists and travelers, the like-minded company she had long sought. These rejuvenating verdant experiences led her to move upstate in 1941, to the loving home of Elmer and Pauline ("Dai") Newton on Rockledge Road (now Rockledge Lane) in the town of Saranac Lake, New York. She wrote to her mother that while plunging down a ski slope, she was reminded "of Auden at his most lyrical" and that poetry "had at last restored to her that balance I knew as a child."

One summer day in 1941, Murray returned to Saranac

Lake from a solitary walking trip in Vermont with a fever and was taken to General Hospital. What seemed to be a fever caused by an infection from a blister instead turned out to be a general infection spreading from her heart. Murray spent the last five months of her life between the hospital and her home at Saranac Lake. She was nursed by her mother and Dai, and visited often by the Jacksons, especially her cousin Jean. Murray died on January 4, 1942. Following her wishes, Peggy, Dai, and Jean spread her ashes at the foot of the pines at St. John's in the Wilderness Episcopal Church in Paul Smiths, a hamlet north of Saranac Lake, reciting her untitled poem that began: "It is not I who am sleeping in the rock under the wood."

After the Yale edition fell into the dustbin of history, it wasn't until John Ashbery published an article on Murray in the October/November 2003 issue of *Poetry Project Newsletter* that her work began to be noticed again in poetry circles. (Ashbery had also mentioned Murray in passing as a "central poet" in his book *Other Traditions*, published in 2000.) In February 2014, Mark Ford's superb essay "Joan Murray and the Bats of Wisdom" appeared in *Poetry* magazine. In it he describes a trunk full of Murray's original manuscripts supposed to have been lost in transit when Peggy sold her own papers, along with her daughter's, to the Smith College archive in 1968. Ford inquired about the trunk and it was subsequently found, complete with a dent in its side, which corroborates the lore of its falling off the delivery truck. But what it contained was still a mystery as the materials had not been processed. Ford's momentous homage to Murray and the bolstering promise of the trunk electrified me with purpose. I visited the archive at the Sophia Smith Collection in September 2014, and had the rare and exhilarating privilege of being the first to go through the new acquisitions, the long-lost papers of one of my favorite poets.

The new materials comprised a tremendous addition to her already astonishing output: the hundreds of pages of missing original manuscripts of poetry; several hundred pages of letters that unlock her previously scant biography and include her correspondence with Auden, as well as reflections on her poetics; about a dozen stories, at least one of which looked like a novella or the novel that she had abandoned, as well as a few short plays in various stages of completion; and the unfinished memoir of her childhood. Lastly, and perhaps the most singularly fascinating manuscript, was an almost four-hundred-page multi-genre autobiographical work that Grant Code compiled from all the materials listed above and dedicated to Peggy. Most if not all of Murray's biography that I've pieced together comes from this text that Code titled *A Faun Surmising*.

In preparing this collection of Murray's poems for New York Review Books, I knew I'd need to pick up where Code had left off as the original editor of the 1947 edition of *Poems*. In his editor's note, Code accurately describes the papers that Murray's mother passed on to him as a "confusion: pages of prose mixed with pages of verse and scarcely two pages of anything together that belonged together." And yet, it is a well-known saga of women's literary history that editors have "improved" or "corrected" their original writings according to their own agendas and perceptions of public taste. Code was well aware of this issue, writing in his note: "I am opposed to the practice of trying to 'improve' the work of poets, as was done with the poems of Emily Dickinson. The important thing is to preserve exactly what the poet wrote."

Code's effort to "prepare the poems for publication," however, competed with his desire "to preserve exactly what the poet wrote." He made frequent changes to grammar and diction in order "to make the meaning and syntax clear." The punctuation he added is far more numerous and regulating of syntax than in even Murray's most revised poems, where the punctuation became much sparser. Perhaps misreading Murray's fluidity and innovation, he shaped single-stanza poems into quatrains and changed neologistic compounds like "greyskirts," "tallgaunt," and "summerwheat" into two words or hyphenated them. Furthermore, because a clear final draft was rarely evident, Code's approach was often to combine "the best of all versions," merging drafts and supplanting the preferred variants, and to add titles to poems that Murray had left without them. He also omitted more than eighty poems considered "incomplete, fragmentary, or immature," granted with some pressure from Auden to do so.

Still, it's hard not to admire Code's tireless efforts to present what he thought would be the best version of Murray's work. Most of her poems exist in multiple typed drafts with no indication of their order of composition or of a preference for one version over another. What look like obvious spelling errors, typos, and formatting inconsistencies abound, sometimes making the text or handwritten edit over the text illegible. Given the absence of a final type-script, trying to understand Murray's composition process automatically becomes open to interpretation. The debt to Code cannot be overstated. Not only did he create an index and manuscript based on what he discerned to be the complete poems, ordering the drafts, typing up clean copies, and creating a variorum edition that included the text of each poem with appended variants from other drafts, but he also typed true copies of her correspondence, organizing them into several volumes totaling more than six hundred pages, alongside his editing of *A Faun Surmising*. Code also put together a supplementary guide to Murray's poetry that Auden vetoed from inclusion in the Yale edition.

After studying Murray's papers—alive with her slanted scrawl and hosts of doodles—I discovered that the differences between the drafts of each poem weren't significant enough to alter a single one. Instead, I considered each individual poem in its relation to the drafts and to the patterns of edits I noticed among all of her poems, and I selected for publication that which appeared to be furthest developed. Though my choice of a "final draft" often agreed with Code's sequencing of the drafts, my decision to let the draft stand as is departs from his editorial approach. If Murray had noted handwritten changes on the typed "final draft," I tried my best to decipher and include these edits, and kept to the typed text where I was otherwise unsure. In the appendix, I've also included notes related to the following: typed words that were illegible and required my best guess; unusually significant changes between drafts, such as adding or dropping a whole stanza, the variant of which I also include in the note; and obvious spelling errors or choices that seemed questionable, which I fixed, as Murray in her letters often voiced her weakness as a speller whenever she found herself writing without a dictionary.

I've preserved Murray's formatting and punctuation exactly as it appeared in the typed manuscripts. While Murray probably would have fiddled further with the punctuation on many of these poems, I wanted to let the poems stand as they are, as much as possible, rather than channel edits. In this spirit, too, all untitled poems are left without titles and signified by their first line in quotes.

I've arranged *Drafts, Fragments, and Poems* into three main sections. The first section consists of a restored version of the complete Yale edition. Code had divided this book into five parts—I have omitted these divisions but preserved his thoughtfully arranged sequence, which clusters certain poems that speak to one another, foregrounds some of Murray's core themes, and considers her development as a poet in relation to the diverse forms she explored. The second includes a small sampling of Murray's extraordinary correspondence, arranged chronologically and drawn from her most active years as a poet, as well as a brief prose piece on her reading habits. The last section, "Drafts, Fragments, and Poems," comprises unpublished poetry that I've gathered from her papers, those poems that I felt best represent the vast chorus of Murray's singular talents. Lastly, the appendix reprints Auden's original foreword to the Yale volume of 1947.

◆ ◆ ◆

Though Murray was a self-professed perfectionist, she distinguishes between a pejorative "neatness" and "balance." The latter signals an erotic feat—when divisions inherent in one's self intertwine. To be vulnerable to both continual destruction and creation and still participate in the work of the building spirit is Murray's invincible realization as a poet. The luxuriance of her uncontainability is there, in what is left unfinished, hanging in the balance. Her quavering lines—whether in scrawls, doodles, or poems—are drawn in heat. Her margins, like her poem's churches, are filled with devils that look like monks (or vice versa) chained and doubling as if in sex magick. Her spiritual architecture is "Unemployed" and "universal"—free from the "second- or third-hand reaction generally exhaled," the doors of perception cleansed. In the poem recited in the pines at the spreading of her ashes, Murray says, "I have no memory to inflict unless I may sing to you." To us, dear readers, the door opens to hear her.

I am deeply grateful to Shanna Compton for championing Murray's poems and for bringing them back to the living, and to Mark Ford for his seminal essay on Murray and for his encouragement in pursuing this project.

I am indebted to the Sophia Smith Collection archivists and staff at Smith College for three years of support, especially to Karen Kukil, whose generous conversations about her monumental work editing Sylvia Plath's original manuscripts were invaluable. Their exquisite attention to the work in their care sustained and inspired me to no end.

Likewise, I am grateful to Edward Mendelson for his expert advice and example of dedication as a scholar and editor of Auden's work. I am grateful to all of NYRB for shepherding Murray's work into print, and in particular to Edwin Frank, Sara Kramer, Karla Eoff, and especially to Jeffrey Yang for his patient and enthusiastic support.

This book almost dedicates itself—to the memory of John Ashbery, one of the most generous, constant proponents of writers of unclassifiable "other traditions," Murray among them. Ashbery raised the bar for all poets to pay closer attention to the young, forgotten, or unsung. His conversations with me about the manuscripts, his love for the fragment and the deceptively "minor" poem, illuminated my editorial path and are reflected in the selection.

For keen and kind attention to the work, thank you to Christine Hume, Mónica de la Torre, Yovana Milošević, Danniel Schoonebeek, Daniel Poppick, Tenaya Nasser-Frederick, Lauren Clark, Alan Felsenthal, and Amaranth Borsuk.

I am most grateful to Joan Murray. This book is especially for all young women poets who see themselves in her.

—*Farnoosh Fathi*

Poems

(1947)

◆ ◆ ◆

If, here in the city, lights glare from various source,
Look out of your window, thin faced man.
Three portent cities repeat the pattern and the course
That history ran.

Three slender veins, clotted and ambiguous,
Are these inlocked hands.
Three startled cries now rise incredulous,
Where once sprang barren sands.

Give back height to receding sky.
Let stars—the things that remain—
Orbit their quiet to the lie
That is here city and various city pain.

This Makes for War!

Do not say the cluttered mass unheaped about the street,
Is not as it should be—
Or the rows and squares and blare of passing objects, not as
    it should be.
Paris, New York, London and the meetings on Fleet
Street. The heat, the smell and its ill effects—
Who objects?

In the spring I have my land—my crocus coming up.
There is complaining as there is wind.
Sitting in the morning and in the evening, complaining as
    there is wind.
A woman with unpinned hair—a moaning dog to disrup-
t the moderate time, the sleepers weaving.
Inevitable evening.

A million clocks talk out across the city.
People angle on along the way.
The ugly baggage and the cripple, (always the cripple!)
Angle on along the way
With us who are the other people, the neat, the sly, the witty;
The men that bit and knew the face of Eve's tart surface apple
Walk on beside the cripple

You think you complain of the ugliness of people.
Meet your own bed
Smell what you said
Your words unmitigated dead
Sink like a noon sun in the crass tomb beneath the steeple.

Two feet above the sand look down
A tartan shore
A clan, a clack, a whore,
A mobile open door
To the dog against the tree, the brittle mugging clown.

Claws like tumbled fingers here
Stand for hands
Elastic bands
Minds and trends
Thighs sprout here enough to breed the honour of your
Morganatic leer.

◆ ◆ ◆

There's a small tale I'd like to tell you here. A bit sad I
   believe.

Not too sad!

There was a little man and his action must be jerked
By a series of mental strings and attitudinizings.
He used to a small little pub somewhere near Whitehall.
Down a drear dark street when his wage came to him he
   would go
And there he would imbibe the raw stuff and rub his hands
   willy

WILLy-NILLy

And later his feet on the floor not speaking or lifting his
   eyes
But living in a strange and bell-clear world of his own
Till the hour struck home.

Why and why you'd ask. Why if he hadn't he would have
   reason

Each morning with the blank walls and the bleak yard
   moaning at him
And he would have said to himself "How wise I am," a
   chuckle here.
"What shades and pleasantries my life must possess.
I must thank all the high swing of things for the clock that
   ticks
The drip of the tap and the sound of the kettle

That whistles up my shilling's gas and whistles up my tea
    too.
Look here's the bread and here's the fine limp book I've
    read.
O I'm a sensible fellow and a practical bit of a lad.
I'm not dead to gentle satyr for I'm conscious of other me
And smile and sigh away their anthropological
    shortcomings.

O wise little man!
I can hear and see and cull the meats
And am at least three-quarters alive to the wonders of the
    space
Moulder and star spinner
Where he leans checkmating the irrelevant with the
    irreverent

The seed with infinity.

I'm so sensible that I simply won't be O won't be O will
    not O
Here the little man leaped up and down though he had the
    black
Hat and black gloves on.

I believe the day was Sunday!

Sunday you know. He might have cried out in the dark
    street.
A thousand rilling years this was his dream
To break through himself. To do something beautifully
That was against the turn of the very stars and know the
    reality
Of the lightest of his piped illusions.

He would sit down thoughtfully afterwards. "It was wrong
    to do that"
                      Here he'd chuff his hands together.
"Or rather indeed how very calm I feel a simple innocence
    holds
me for verily I was proclaimed an angel. I saw the little gods
stirring themselves in their own day after beds."
But the truth was the poor little devil had been run over
Dead in the street in his Sunday best.

◆ ◆ ◆

Three men sat at a millstone table
One looked up, one down one about
And they were one head and a fable
Spin the millstone spin the millstone out
For the mind of the men spoke in it
At the millstone was themselves in allwise
The large and the small of them sit
With shiny elbows and backs that fall and rise
As they breathe out and into the table
All the energies of a life times thought
On the weight of an object and analyzed fable
Bundle well in the hard knotty thoughts in this spot

They played by the water Chuck, Mink, Stode,
And the Fat Jew fellow with the nose
Strutted the glitter of a wagon lode
Pink, striped candied, lemon froze
Up by the avenue east river junk
Old shops a dirt colour cabbage king
Eating bread and eating cheese in one big hunk
Old Pascal cabbage king breaks in swing
Fat Jew turns his head "Igh Paggli!"
Play by the water Chuck Mink stode
River rattlets with railthin thighs
Sandy haired bandy kneed strode
White trousers flapping gob hat sea eyes
Sandy Sam on leave on land!
Old man sits in the sun and blinks
Strokes his beard and his sons been canned
Pulls at the yellow white threads and thinks
And the Sandy young fellow and the jew

And the cabbages king of the avenue east
They don't know but himself he knew
What it's like to be old like a rabbi priest
Chuck Mink Stode run from the river
Over to second and third and the shop
"Ikey" and "Ikey" and give us a sliver
Or bread from Pascali with a handspring and hop
Or dime from the swell guy the Gob Gob Gob.
All home to supper Chuck Mink Stode
Fine far jew fellow looks at the sun
Up with the glittering gilt on with the lode
Young Mr. Sandy Sam off to meet the Hon'
Pasqually cabbage king and garlic in the nose
Off for a great spaghetti turns to close up
Hurries the shutter down takes the apron from the cloths
Old man sits rocking in his small black hat
Old man sits rocking in dusk!

◆ ◆ ◆

The Oblique chapels of the Gothic,
Blink with a dim prenatal distinction.
The querulous beam, championing through the thick
Spumey scent, quibbles the dark with some elation.

And the passions of night are out
And the slippery imp chuckling at eaves,
Where the moss gargoyles let the useful spot
Of mouth suck in thirst and then relieve.

The devil and the flesh spank thighs,
Duck from sight and torture down the aisle,
Accosting prayers and sighs
Heightening the drab pale monks each in their militant file.

The in and out of God has lapped such vital tears,
And now the necromancers and Mongol apes
Tear at the crisp blue air and use their fears
For bolts and doors, their skins for capes.

Within the niche the sterile eyed Madonna screened,
Apostles chipped and overdressed,
But lovely in the meaning of the preened
Undulating beards all abundantly well blessed.

Mongoloid fool, your saffron seasick face
Will do no harm to women to children
A fangy slit-eyed creature of non-race
Perversion from true fact, the natural spleen of men.

In the chapel they will nurture and condone you,
Put you in striped pants and high fool's hat
Teach sordid pity and lust in the more than casual few,
Then gibber and bang your blunt hands flat,

Against the inundated void that is more devil
More sucking pity, black, sleep tasting.
Gothic chapels watch the steeple, the squinting gargoyles
    spill
Fools breed in aisles the somnambulant monks strictly
    castrating.

◆ ◆ ◆

The starved houses without brinks or people
Wander about the desolate streets.
Little boys would have stained their corners yellow
And old wives cherished their stoops.

The architect counts his ribs the house its bone.
The window frames distend emphatic day concave night:
The attempt to shape and lay the air is done.

It is the young architect in the old village
And with what trepidity he reaches for a time
Dizzy with starved action handles clay,
Threads with the slightest over-dream a city
Planned with a bird upon each bow a light upon each face.

The neat Sunday family directs its walk toward church
The airplane and lark comment upon the weather
The home, a jove, spring each its living wisdom,
Old men with pipes click dry thumbs on round bowls,

The nightmare of empty houses in retreat,
The lovely unwanted with drafting board upon his knee
Glares at the grave placement of nursery and kitchen
Measure each each to the fragile scale of starved necessity.

The Builder

1

It is the action of the water that is the nearest thing to man.
That is what the young of the people cried, lifting their
Heads from the work they had turned to with indolence.

2

"Crack at that pile, young fellow," went up the sullen cry.
"No time to stop in the work and the job only time to
    breathe
And breathin' your own fine sweat, for the air's too good
For a world to stop us for, us for, us for!"

3

High scuttle of dying leaves in fall like a dab and a stain
And the colour to words that are dreamed in the head.
Spring prancing up like a dainty colt
Picking the place for its feet, and lilies work up from its
Feet.

4

O I want to wander over the hills and down to the water
And if there is sea I want to pack it up to my arms
And let the blue globe of all that water fill in my mouth
Rill up my head, my chest, burst out of the sullen seed of
    my loin.

5

Crack at that pile, young fellow, went up the sullen cry
We're making towers of Babel, that babble and Babel
We're building towers of Babel that will crumble down
     before dawn.

The man who smiles and totters with the riveter
Throws the red rivet through the paupered air
Is more than the simple statement or young inventor
Glaring with spectacles from the brain's cramped lair

He waves a hand with its brisk intelligible symbol
The facts are his children not the plans
His wife has a face as still as the grave upon the knoll
Where the women clap and stand to wait for every man.

Twirling between girders and the night
The man who smiles like and lights the cigarette
Nods to another day and wishes for a child of his delight
A quick reflex admits the brawn the brain the infant
    intellect

◆ ◆ ◆

Sleep little architect it is your mother's wish
That you should lave your eyes and hang them up in dreams
Into the lowest sea swims the great sperm fish
If I should rock you the whole world would rock within
    my arms

Your father is a greater architect than even you
His structure falls between high Venus and far Mars
He rubs the magic of the old and then peers through
The blueprint lies the night the plan the stars.

You will place mountains too when you are grown
The grass will not be so insignificant the stone so dead
You will spiral up the mansions we have sown
Drop your lids little architect admit the bats of wisdom in
    your head.

◆ ◆ ◆

Night rising from sleek coils a snake in the house of the
    Architect
And the breath of the sleeper rising and the window where
    leaves
Gather
And the insect repeating in sound the monotonous still
    the stars inflict
Upon the changeable vision of the night mind and its
    flutter.

In the hour when the mother has become an eye in sleep
Over the palm of the cold the woman stirs and it is her
    own hand
She draws to all the breathing leaves the deep
Sea tone that means to their tired weight their salt
    beginning and ultimate end.

The Woman tugs from the scent what the memory of
    space intends
Only to be grasped by those who are white with time and
    tide
And she expands into the City where the wall extends
Both up and down and yet seems neither narrow high or
    wide.

The house of the Architect and the archaic symbol of dark
Cry for the dance of the wandering optimism
O stir with your memory of a stark
Hand opening like a flower upon the mock action of rock
    cataclysm

Work in Progress

Look to your hands life of rare genuflection,
The wind has a strange destruction
Upon leaves of trees, and look to your feet,
Where walking is done the winter cares little about the neat
Step; and look to all that is yours,
So that we who will to possess may not call you ours.
Learn from the indifference of the land
To draw back from the drooped lids and the wavering
   demand.
A child's face is a peculiar thing where it does not belong.
What mature mind would turn to a wrong
Act? Therefore, look to your hills and your sun,
Gather aside the walks and the ways where the wild deer
   run.

◆ ◆ ◆

There are shapes out of the North.
That you are of the prow of the Iceland;
That your face is the Kelt and the North,
As the race and the brief shores hard-swept sand.

Brittle spoors of the sea in strange environment
That is your step; a colloquial murmur that is your being.
Scud then from the obsolete into a new wind's abandonment
Or cut at the sea sperm calculated to draw you into a
    nightmare's scheming.

Only remember this:—of all things that tread well,
You tread splendidly along the route.
Earth and tide, age of the mountain, the lift and swell;
These are the shapes of you the waves dispute.

◆ ◆ ◆

You talk of art of work of books
Have ever sat down thought all that's to do
That book to read that book to write
Sat down stood up walked back and forth
Because not an action you could do would
Fill the gap that's wanting action to the chin
Look look into the past one damn moment
Out of a thousand years one infinite moment
And on that you ask me to work to dream to do
Try it yourself on nothing I can't
Every confounded one has had so much of life
That left gasping in a stinking or a lighter air
Left out of breath and glad to think at last
Higher or lower their there and there and there
And I where am I where I began where I'll end
Sitting sitting with the last grail of will
Rotting in time and there's no time or tide in me
You talk of art of work of books
I'll talk of nothing in its lowest state
Talk till my jaw hangs limply at the joint
And the talk that's one big yawn in the face of all of you
Empty as head empty as mood and weak
And I can hear all the watery wells of desolation
Lapping a numbing sleep within the head

◆ ◆ ◆

What can I do Methuselah your time is mine
Without reason but with flattened sheets
Sheets wrapping corpses or sheet sky
White with that blue tired undertone
I am here with arms arms asking without voice
For voices cannot always say something from the middle
From the stomach that is empty or even lift lips
Delicate crescent lip cannot speak loudly loudly
But only mute when all the heart has driveled out
And O I am here alone now it has all birds
In flutter and in nail curved distances again
What to say what to say that only arms can say it
Wrap corpses in a sheet of cooler evening sky
Corpses of even shroud illusion as is emptiness
Here here with cherrycoloured scarfs
I wrap my mistressthoughts with wider arms
Rolling her eyes upon my oustretched palms
Till the hours grow and the lowflung beard of night
Has wedged itself between another mood
Down the thousand years you shuffle back the corridors
Twinkle a pale rimed curve of the lips
What can I do Methuselah without the wisdom of
Your laughter
Give me a cockerel heaven so that I may crow to
The turn of your rising smile!

Ascetic: Time Misplaced

1

Drive your rod with a consistence down
Striking the cold black loam,
Till with a flourish and a sudden cry
One thin strand of infinitesimal leaf,
Stark in its beginning as a simple touch
Made to feel about the splendid earth
Palming the hand here there and everywhere,
One infinitesimal leaf leaps up.

2

I have seen hills and rhythm
Will not leave my head.
I have seen, since I was a pink and cottoned
Little thing,
Leaves with the brimming sun spilt down.
I have thought myself into Pan
And run with Sappho after women's feet.
Hated the stuff that makes all life
For the very slough and insect breed of it.
I have made the asses of the flatlands bray
kicking their hooves up in the thistled brake.
Dreamed to drink with gods and puttered
In a frenzy with those less than mortal.
I have dreamed and dreamed myself to life
And back again
And now with my body fat my brain irresolute
I see nothing once again but nothing
Only the bloom of an impeccably quiet dust.

On Dit!

If I had spent whole nights watching you,
Gutting the candles in as many winks
I would be Pharisee or utter hypocrite,
Whichever pleased to put your mind at ease.
I call myself illusion all transgressional
There's little pity rollicked here for me.
I know the very truth of action is at surface
A string pulled in the outward throw of things.
By heaven take the cake I'll take one too!
Lecherous thoughts and puritanical rub grey,
But never mind, even if grey's the basis for decline
We'll take the cake and swim the Hellespont of time
And if my Hellespont should be a gutter-swell
Remember me to Lucifer.
But come, there's so much rot in that collapse
For what am I but I whether the conscience
Turns to mud or passes to a more ambiguous state.
I shall be I quite still beside the night,
Dreaming Samaritan rolling small pills of wax
Dropped by the candles and the hours.

Ego Alter Ego

I am watching you as you stand,
A child of riddles in the head
Of thoughts that rill in circles
Big and little prick with doubt
The fault turned always in.
What I could do or say lies here
In my smile and in my anger
In my wonder at your consciousness
That always answers every why
With an ironic answering smile
Twisting the full flesh of your lips.
Stand before me let down your lids
Now let your body lean against
The warm before noon rocks
Listen to the slavering of the waves
Mouthing along the shore
And feel that I am that receptacle,
Here where I lie machete naked
An imprint in the shadow,
That I am an independent void
Absorbing into my wisdom and my mind
All that you have to give in words
Hoping in the simplicity of my listening
You may forget eternal self.
We scrambled down these rocks together
And your eyes were blue candor circles,
Child's eyes and enigmatic for me.
I wondered if this was you
When looking up I saw you looking down
You without place or sex
Quiet and with the first clear idea

Awakening to yourself with wings.
The stoop of a gull swinging out
In one wide taking in had caught you
And you were that quiet nothingness.
One could put up one's hand
And grasp the hollowglass of sky
Rattling the gulls against the sides
And the scratch of their cry
Flipping them back and forth
Like motes of pollen to the wind
Without end and without beginning.
O the benevolence of space
There, the graciousness of motherhood
The full breast and the sucking
And the man against her knees
The great abstract growth of space.
We are so young you and I
People pointing whisper amongst themselves
"Too young, too young for such an age!"
And then like rubble rubbling down
The Embankment to splash noisily
All "Child child eternal child!"
And so the river carries on the words
We are so young you and I
And beyond the dustbowls
Even golddust stings or so they say
Stings in the every strength ... illusion
But come stand before me ... speak
Stand where the sun is warmest
I have seen, when walking here,
That trees perpendicular stand,
White, implacable, coolbarked;
Little to say and whispering, well said,
As all small simplicities grow large

In voicing all so simply.
I shall catch her between these stems
Running all day beside the running water.
Watch how it slips into concave shadows,
Streams with the music that belongs and here.
To her this is the right completion
For sounds, like fawns filled with their own surprise
Leap to her her sides and running,
Leap from her lips, her snarled smile
Never caught, never held, leafblown.
Leaves crumpling, shivered in the hand
Are all that I have held.
Weep Diana more than that you could not be
For she lingering between barked stem and stem
Where water running faster, faster leapt
Strained me toward her and my eyes
Surreptitiously raised drift emptily
Amongst tangled lights and drift.
I think we shall sit and weep Diana
You and I for a moment.

To W. H. Auden

You, held in the thin cusp of the night,
Capped by unevenly placed stars,
Rocking yourself like a blond char knowing tomorrow's
    labour,
Or today's soldier as he shouts and mars
The sleek dragon, having been put to flight
Once too often before its enigmatic horrour.

We have seen you as a man with strange possibilities,
As a child with odd angularity and slumped,
And we have and have not denied you your sensitivities.
We have seen you on fields humped
And at various leisure reaching for flowers we knew,
And turning with nervous fingers shells upon rocks we knew.

London alleys and bus tickets snapped at Piccadilly
With the soot and the rain and the wind let loose....
We have watched you amble there without maturity,
Flung between candescent thoughts on land that killed the
    goose
Destined to lose the golden egg, this island that we knew,
This river, this Embankment, this power for the few.

No more may you grasp out from your window
Than you have stroked, heard or broken,
In the days and hours of your pain
Your mind now flexed and lean in the archives of the spoken
To be the slant sphinx whose thought the sands repudiate
    and blow,
Or the wide hurt that shows dark earth and flowers after rain.

The Young Host of Rockledge

Over Saranac even the lights have gone,
The dark guests flick silver candles with a star.
Over the sparsely peopled town, the narcotic snow, one
Unseen figure after another puts out a hand far
To the crackling rim of mountain and breaks bread.
The wind for a brief moment sniffs the snow of sleep,
Blowing it high to the sterile sleek sky of the winter dead.
The multitudes of two and two keep
Watch in a slender shape of birch and hemlock and the
    larch.
Quietly we each taste at the corner of a different thought.
The woman, lovely as all things must be, sits with the
    fearful march
Of the insect and the stars within her head, forever caught,
Forever wound in the delicate web of the hidden spider.
The man, the host, smiling slowly turns about
Till we see the oblique church figuring the eyes and mask
Of the eternal stranger.
A hand across the face and lids shakes out
And down onto the table the still New England dust.
The guests nod, whispering between the unblown flames.
Far beyond night the vacant dreaming quiet moves from
    a space absorbing lust
To answer the queries of a little child and play the old
    glad games.
We see the real host of the house and why the tall trees
    stand,
And the unseen guests draw three full seas of laughter from
The eye:
The son of the house demands a silver snow upon a
    summer strand!

What had been brooding in a faithless sleep leaped from
the table with a thin birds-cry.

Poem: For Dai

As the summer sun comes down into the autumn trees,
And we feel the hills to be drums between the knees
Of the phlegmatic Indian depositing his thought by beat;
And we advance under the birch and hemlock or retreat
With our factual minds hunting the winter place,
I think we would not forget our one brief act in space.

The mathematical scar has alarmed or delighted us.
We break with many fingers the uncertain truce
Between the ledge and the vegetable earth,
Dividing our appetites according to their worth.
Somewhere the satisfaction lies in the shy animal,
A moment touching grass, the next, leaping the enigmatic
    wall.

We cannot incantate without the leaves or wind;
We could not turn to each other with crying at an end,
Or make the gestures of the mind a fact,
If we had not conceived of the extraordinary act
That recurs like the wandering race, the day and season,
And the woman who forever hums the name of an
    unnatural son.

The terrible legend disporting with the night
Sends the birch and pine in tiers of shivering flight
Over the climate of the hills descending to the valley;
While we remain all quiet in that remarkable memory,
Our minds extending through a fragmentary space
To grasp the implication of the drum that speaks the thought
Of the inverted face.

❖ ❖ ❖

Here we stand before the temporal world
And whether we care to cast our minds
Or shiver our worlds of all that refutes
The clarity of thought
Whether we wish to deflect the rudiments of source
Bear bastard brats in something up the whole
These things I do not know
Words have been to me like steps
Revolving and revolving in one cell
Perhaps others have felt the limit of the pendulum
Looking to the vast confines of night
And conscious only of the narrow head
The brief skull imminent of life
Grey granules that like time run through the hours.

Caesar walked quietly in his garden
Two scribes walked gravely at his side
The smooth pink marble of the fluted column passed
Reminded him of warm wine from the grapes
The glitter of a spear dropped carelessly
And caught by a hand quicker than he could see
Its slanting fall
Reminded him of the shallow eyes that glinted
As he passed between two worlds their own and his.
His thoughts tended toward irrelevance
But his words cut out the veriest patterns
Of an eastern drive toward the steeples of far Babylon

You Spoke of Windmills

It is Quixotic to be fighting Windmills.
In my inevitable surrealism not even hills
Could be more than the narrow ledge of illusion—
And my fat Panza donkey—sitting to the exclusion
Of anything but donkey sitting.

Always a gilt knight against a pluméd sky,
(Malleable reference in the sense to cap-a-pie!)
A Dulcinea to facilitate the soul,
And so one struts through times including role,
Even if tomorrow is, while yesterdays move out.

You spoke of Windmills where the mind parades,
You clipped your words with the worth that truth
    engraves.
Yet, know the vast aloneness of this Don,
A querulous soldier, a life's inveterate Pawn—
As sensible in his brave dream as we are not.

The Long Trail

I have been marking the long high roads.

I think it was over the trail
That angles on riddling the mountain wood
Up and down in the cool musk valleys
Up and up to the height where blue and drawn
The reaches and the farther hills
Turned their great shadows and grave lines
To more than form to more than opulent colour.

Poem

Three mountains high,
O you are a deep and marvelous blue.
It was with my palms
That I rounded out your slopes;
There was an easy calmness,
An irrelevant ease that touched me
And I stretched my arms and smoothed
Three mountains high.

♦ ♦ ♦

Things that are sinuous are the rivers of the land
Women stalking with the ripple of cats
Along the leg and movement of the body
In deep eddies in silk transparencies.
Rivers of the tumbled slopes
The flatlands to the west
Tidal-rivers licking and drawing back
The whole weight of protuberance toward the sea.
Marking a salt ridge in the bright flush of the flats.
O sea grasses waving in the high of a quickened
Sea grass wavering in the high flush of the flats.
They are women with the bare and subtle feet
Of brooks or rills of mountain lakes
Of turbulent cascades of torrential moments
Of long coil tenuous drift with one still cloud
Sucking from rim to rim of that insoluble thing
It was down to the river and the beat of the river

Not that I had ever laughed too much
Beside the million mile looped river
Turning its course with slug trepidity
Toward my dangled fingers
I came to smile berserkly at the dawn
Forcing my self to lie here by this river
Shaping a pocket in the shrill damp air
To warm my sides along
Now even the smile has gone and I am face to face
With the insoluble riddle of the moment
Hold myself empty and mistily reflected
In the jade grey water
River them river whole times to sensation
Water dip dipping to the fingertips
And in the touch a bird's diminuendo transcendental
Masticated to the new reality
I came to smile at dawns because I thought it just
Now I momently relieve such strain
By throwing back my lids to free my eyeballs
Relaxing the body to strain perception
God river your thoughts I'll river mine and here
There's nothing to ask but clouds about the head
Wind winnowed grasses in the hair and blown
Down the stirring water
More finely felt more more aspirant to nuance
That is the finite shading that reveals the whole
Now smiling and now laughing beside the stream of
    river
Exquisitely conscious of the selfadvent

◆ ◆ ◆

Like a wind passing slowly along the valley
That which passes by is narrow and is the woman
Is the autumn leaf leaped between one tree
And long looning of one bird to scan
One tree one land one river in no hour.

Pools where evening leaves rattle fan whipped
On water on the backs of tilting drakes
And the dry throat unmossed of up ripped
Up leached rocks pools that gather into lakes
Inlocked world whose blue hills edge between

So down to the treed dark plain from height
Like a wind passing slowly along the valley
So many women move Indian eyed and light
With far walking and knowledge of freely
Swept and

Drought

Drought, what inscrutable mask
Over the fragile over the musk—
Over all these green hills
That once filled their sides and valleys
With innumerable lacerate pools.
Fish with tails unminted
Their silver surface hollowed
Under the springs flood stones
Over the rumpled dry stream;
Their bones laced to the bed
And mouths V'd wide unbreathing.

The Exiles

The day we stood as people stand
Looking out towards the land,
We were lovers of things beyond our bodies.

We were grave women, simple men;
With less than a turn we knew it then:—
A place, a land, a cliff as silver as bitten sea.

Without a stir we straddled our minds
Into remembered outer rinds—
River and height and the outflanked shore.

The long keen stride on the plow churned earth
Meant with the pain the full year's birth;
While seasons like boys spat seeds against our knees.

Spring

O but there is a laughing spring
Even little men see that
A running through the white board towns signing
A light that glints from painted steeples
A minnow-silver rain
Of all the clouds contain

Spring crackling its buds
Every instant a remark
Each brisk spanked cloud that scuds
A brief out from the invulnerable sun
The sea in May
The barking ivory spray.

These are toetarion energies
It is not soft but direct
It is only the byplay that has its lethargies
The life stamps and commands
It is the little man
That tricks his little span.

O but there is a laughing spring
With its head back and its mouth wide
Its square breasts and masculine wring
In every vaunting stride

There is mountain of energy
A bank and flay of spray
That is tomorrow not torrid lethargy
Not subtle April but turbid May

Willows snap the too smooth slope
The birch knifes through the night
And lilies roar within their fragile scope
Every phase of sweet is put to flight.

Sap goes to the head of it all
In a leaping drunk of remembered winters
Of tattered leaves their embittered fall
Ice to the bone to the heart in jagged splinter.

Spring like a cudgel beating fat out of the land
Waves breaking off of the sand
Swaggering all sex wise and opening the sky
Waves slapping on the hard bruised sand

Vermont and the Hills and the Valleys

1

Tremendous are the ways of the simple people,
The hills speak with their mouths,
The sky laughs out the rims of their eyes,
The earth walks with the feet of the people
And the wind and the dead are their souls awake
And the sleep, that is theirs comes when the eye-lid
Slips down to meet the soiled slant of their cheeks.

2

Great arc the mountain slopes curving along the line
Flanked by the river or the smooth-glint track of train:
A speed of smoke, a sprung-coil loosely heaped beyond the
    span of steel.
Look to right—look to the left and the fields
That fit in languid patterns between trees,
Umber cornstalks, hay in warm-split stacks!

3

Tight is the hair of women who call cows to the milking,
Wrists and fingers playing out the movement of the
    udder-press.
White is the angle and the piss and splash of milk.

Let it be remembered, O, let it be remembered
That these are the women and the simple people!

4

The oxen plow and wagon the hay in its high dung-gold,
Making long horns shape and hold the moon,
The red of their sides squat.
The green of the trees spring in wide green waves to the
    wind,
To the fields and the wide-palmed spread of space.

5

The men are before the night:
With the cracks of their cheeks filled with dust,
And the hands heavy like listless rakes swung down,
And the dirt and sweat on their lips,
And the rise and fall of their chests.

6

The women go from the milking to the pot without
    compunction.
Steps of men and women from the field to the home,
From the plow to the reaping in the deep high swell of
    wheat.

There are the simple people
Whose hands rest still on a Sabbath,
And great are the fields and the mountains,
And great are the slopes and the valleys.

Vermont Journey

1

Momentary lift of plain and sea,
Rib of land and then the sea.
O, the immense sea-rock, the land.
O land that in back time
Moved beyond waves' mad leap or suck.
Deep suck, mouthing rivers!
Plainly the rivers running through
Gutted these cool green throats of valley.

2

Blue Ridge men move their
Slow lean limbs on alien grown,
Muttering with the strange tongue
Of carefully witted people.
Alien men, a mountain of the cast;
Yet axe is sound, a lilting ring,
To those who lift and stroke it clean
On alien or any other land

3

"Men are women!"
The old thinned beards fade
Evening leaves only the circle of porch sitters
With their short-napped beards,
Slow moving satyr strands.
          "Trees flesh to the boy.
He lifts his hand soft,
Like a woman drawing tears

Down and away from the face;
When the leaves fall he weeps,
With the eyes of an old woman."

4
Great flung and measureless steps
And a woman running along,
A dog twisting and pacing at her feet.
She is running dryly with the dog,
Her eyes cutting on beyond the river.

A cool stare through the half dusk,
She meets the memory of the day,
The profit of the milking with its loss.

5
What tales are linked up in this land,
But mountains and the people are equally grave
And the best that's said is brief.

Old Men

The corn is ripe.
I have known the heat to come up a smoke-pot.
The corn is ripe.
I have put out my hand and plucked grass
Put the grass in my mouth and chewed a cud
Spat the cud high in the air
And hit the field lily smack in the centre.
Couldn't do better than that!

There was sea here;
If I breathe deep I can still smell salt earth.
I found two twisted sea-copias once,
I was a boy and I remember how bleached they
    looked
Cool in my earth stained hand.

2

The hay's rust.
The sun is like a quick-sore running.
There should be green hay
The underside of water is the colour I saw.
I used to gather it in great handfuls
And pluck at the soft green beards
Chew at the narrow grass stalks.

When I was a boy I used to go naked in the quarries.
Lift the great white slabs to me.
The sun beat hard my muscles drummed the rhythm
And there was a fine wide sea-search in my head

White marble glare and the glow of my young
    smoothed skin
        But I was a boy then.

3
Rain in the mountains rain to the hills
The cows are moaning late these nights!

Rain in the mountains rain in the hills
The cows are moaning late these nights.
The cows moan still before morning

New England Woman

1

The tall dark sharp-faced woman came to the door
And gave the mop a crack across the rail of the porch.
A dry leaf zig-zagged down between two maples
And blew with a dry crisp patter on the street.

2

The morning had been clear like sweet-honey
And now the autumn sun spilt down amber-deep
And warm about the near trees and the far blue hills.

3

She would have liked rain and the long bleak drizzled days.
When the trees were bare with the last sad leaf turned
A little patterned skeleton on the ground
And there was the cold sleet feeling in the air
That seemed to hold the land.
When the trees were awkward bony things
Scraggling up to a far of stretch of sky and there was
The smallest etch of a crow's black wing and the shrill
Cracked cry.
These were the times and feelings that were made of
The same stuff as her pale face, coiled black hair,
The sharpness of her joints and the brooding of her mood.

4

She gave the mop another crack and went inside.

Mad John

The John rolled back where he was
Grinned a corn-row of teeth at the sky.
The light was a pink mouse run off its feet
Streaming its tail and winding to the sea.
The John sat grinning out about him
Flapping his hands squashed pink on green.
"What did I come for? What did I seen, uh?"
The words plunked and rubbed back into silence.
If the crow had scrawked out to him maybe...
Or a jittering chatter of things had spoke
And spoke out of turn in the wide big flow
But nothing'd answer if he didn't care
                    And he didn't.
The John's a dull, yellow-matted head of a lad
Rolled back to the ground he's lying
With tobacco-smoke in his lung and a cob.
He's snorting down the wind letting go smoke.
And where'll it go when it meets the night
Comes up to night and joins the swell of black?
The John shrugs smacks the green and turns.
All the great weight of him goes round.
"What did I come for? What did I seen, uh?"
He'd ask and turn to grab the first quiet spill of stars.

The Magdelina

1

They had stood expostulating to their God,
Catching the web-grey sky between their thoughts.
Across the fields, with the endless slabs of soil
Turned to the light and the icy-pools eyed up,
These men stared mumbling in bleak stolidity.
I slumped against the drift-fence where I stood.
One lean hand had squared with work about the fingers!
Hands of poets stood out from my arms beside them,
These standing men with incorrigible fists.
The seed of grey-swung women grew to life
Up from the shallow hollows of the land.
Long gaunt strides of the indefatigable land-born,
Well-tempered females, breast and spanned-hip swinging.
The hung-sky sagged toward the higher rise,
Pressing the last echo of a breath beyond the field.
The cold arched and stiffened out to the horizon.

2

A woman was fingering her sides through red cloth.
Her hands dreamed from the wrist in slender-threads,
While the tall gaunt women spread their skirts against her.
The wide mute spread strode strongly with its men
Stepping away the far bells sullen beat.

3

The woman shoved the red cloth from her face.
I turned, for the sun had circled the bent sky
Leaving me in my own shadow so that I must turn,

And turn and turn again to face her.
"My name is Magdelina, and my sides and the sun and
    forever!"
That is where the rivered summer wheat has tangled,
The concentrated desolation of a span!

4
Into the cloudless smooth of space the bells,
Sounds like grey-skirts fluttering to mind.
The men are standing with bared-eyes curled along pages.
The women with the fine weight of their hips in place,
Rock imperceptibly about the high-chant of a hymn.

5
Here there is nothing:
The fence, the mud, the fields dragged stark and undulate,
A few dried leaves whirled red.

Talk of People in Warning

We are green torrents invulnerable,
We are an admixture of trees and the black earth.
Sundays come in dark cloth and all weeks end.
Fishing smacks from Hythe to Perth,
Flatter the sea
With its immensity.

We plow, we back up the day to breaking,
Sackcloth and ashes, sackcloth and ashes.
Not uncomplaining widows on a Sunday.
Now now. Never now. A woman dashes,
Squats in pain,
Remains in pain.

We are faces blackening windows,
Eyes that pass through stone and remember.
Sands that number us, brisk stars to perceive
From the dryboned November,
The seed of us,
Tremulous.

The Song of Things Watching

Do you see lovers?
We see quiet trees together;
Where young men knelt flowers,
Where young girls stood, daughters
Of earth-winding water.

The old father plucks
With the hands of a dry wind.
The old mother clucks
A soft tongue with the rooks
Of sleep attending her mind.

Love reaching night
Stands slender hipped,
Slender fingered in delight,
Not moving to the left or right
Though star tripped.

The marriage bed,
The unborn moment hung,
The thin bone of the dead—
Now brushed the infant head
Where innocents had sung.

An Epithalamium: Marriage Poem for an Age

THE YOUNG WOMEN
We had loved the self, each other and the rounded slope,
For being young abrupt shapes with abrupt words hurt.
Finding we could not know ourselves we turned to catch reflection
And meeting our difference we felt less apart.
Where the shallow hills are curved the rains may run iron ore,
And every heartless height holds some slight green.
Daughters of the Rock-Climbers fumbling in dark valleys,
Naturally drawing from our history, the lean
Unpampered war-cry or keen instructor of immediate action;
Yet we chose an eerie present of not giving, hugging the slope against the shale.
Now our virginity has gone with the first step,
And our minds, allowing growth, have already dreamt the male and female.
These are no longer boys we see but men. We are no longer girls but women.

THE YOUNG MEN
Now we will listen to the long grass and the trees.
More beautiful than our morning song that clapped back from the peak,
Are the things that breathe about us on this day.
We put down our hands and kneel upon the ground to hear it speak,
Return an unpremeditated dream in glad reply.

What is the time and hour? On the hill we see the child
    plucking flowers:
The round face of the day is seeded with infinities.

The round face of the day is seeded with infinities
The children stamp the strict parent the adroit infant cowers
In our minds the children stamp, the parent frowns, the
    infant cowers
Behind the random cluster, the flower symbol, to smother
    laughter.
Compact and kneeling we smooth the wet grass to one side
We are learning to touch the earth with considerations
Learning to touch earth with consideration
Knowing that we must be less militant and young, to
    stroke the things that hide.
Even the bright dew weeps away the stem, at our inept and
    thoughtless touch.

THE YOUNG WOMEN
Fear with us was care. Nature had commended us to life,
And flocking, smiling, nodding we hid our exactions closed
    beneath lids.
Some of us paused, some gambled and unflowered at the
    brink;
Most of us knew cathedral choirs and envisioned noisy
    steeples in our heads:
But now all the images of earth have soared and bedded
    down in space.
Care is the mother of the moment whose arms we drop.
Thrusting blossoms from the face, we open up our eyes
We stare:
Released from our guard we see the night birds swoop
Across the unlidded pool, down to the valleys.

The day is here! Run and lift the small child with its flower.
The little ones have been gathering since the first streak:
The old mouths, tonguing the dawn with remembered
    clatter,
Have not left unblessed our history, the crevice or the crags.

THE YOUNG MEN

Let us speak long on the wooing and our thoughts.
Beside the water each of us strip and take direction
Knowing that we move within a pattern.
Bending our steps alone from the bank to the liquid
Desolation,
We realize that an act of life will fling us through the void;
The spiral of possession whirling us with insensate sound,
That thins at last and pointing out ejects us into quiet.
Marvelous are those stars that hold and the waters that wind
The inert mountains lashed down by the pine and streams.
No lover considering the day of his marriage should ever
    envy the hawk its height!
Turning our minds within the head we anticipate many
Whispers,
In which death extends to life some portion in the brood-
    world of the night.
It is not only the female fact that we meet here, it is the
    river into sea and bared peninsulas.

THE YOUNG WOMEN

Dance while we are young. (There is an old dance of the
    mind)
Articulate all the movements that are mute in step.
The deep mouth of the wind sucks in its breath.
Our skirts are so high in blowing. A little wild are the notes
That keep

In time, that sing out of the past the tune of the deleted
swan.
The betrothed come to us over the flower rabble of the hill.
Glad that we learned to smile, for laughter would have
tired us
And tears appeared to be denial of the will,
We took all the variations of the self and pressed about the
one;
Till every particle of fact was faced and we were not
wine-sick on love,
Not laughter-ridden or tear-dazed; but strangely open
In a mood that strained to understand and not reprove.
O wind, put down the skirt! Let us fold our hands, be firm
and neat.
The Puritan poised in brief cracks the placid pond,
And we would not remind the correct back or the tight
beak of our
Wedding night.
If some of us have stretched upon grass for other hearts to
'tend,
More have turned up pebbles or shouted down the vacant
channels of dark wells.

THE YOUNG MEN
We mount the irregular land and halt the advance,
As people expanding into dreamt of but unmapped
country.
Only by the celt and sign the earth work and the roads
Shall we give imaginary form to the early inhabitant, and
the free
Intrepid race. You have said that yours was the heritage of
the rock climber.
Together we will give the seed and fruit that grows explicit
in its step

Rejecting no light or shade: but leaping from crag to slope
in the
Sun,
Drumming with heels on earth, the head on the rim of day:
till the inanimates weep,
Generations hold their pain with knowledge of impending
laughter,
The wide become unfathomable and the parent, stiff with
history,
Exerts the spirit of the future in the child.
Room for the irrelevant allows our act of love its mystery,
In which the cult of nights abound and images of life take on
The attitudes of sleep.

THE YOUNG WOMEN
Look into our eyes for there is nothing there unknown.
At every turn we see some black direction that grows grave
with light.
We pity those who lift back the morning and sink into a
welt of barren dark
Where there is no deviation from lasting end in sight.
Here is the harvest, the hand extending, a floor to the sea
the air above.
We are not waters to be drowned in, nor have we under
rocks for
Wrecking.
Where storms are you have met our temper, the crackle of
high leaves
Our talk,
Our love is a whip to winter wind and our rest the corn
clinging
Over the sound acres of a civilized land.
What wisdom can we bring you that we have not found
together?

Each morning we wake up out of the same mother place,
With the same animal blinking as the lizard, paused and
    neuter,
Before discovering ourselves and then our shape.
Our life is a nakedness moving through tormented weather
    with a will.
Living with man we cannot be apart from any fraction of
    the
Kind.
Come, O, come to us now so that we shall know more of
    the strict pine on the hill,
Lovers may touch but the marriage bond is a link without
    distraction

◆ ◆ ◆

There is a rocky jut, flung like a disc
Against the dull dim roll of sea and sky.
I have heard, I have heard of the place,
And now I see it from the walls of a city
Choked with rubble and the thoughtless
Droppings of the curlews nesting the brood,
And playing their wings with the whim of the wind
In the streams and rills of the air.

The sea is a slate, impenetrable as steel
That the birds dent and rebound from
With listless monotony of movement.
As I gaze from the cracked and broken pane
Of an old stained window of the desolate church,
My eyes reaching the light
Between the dull flutter of thought that rebounds
Like the cry and the proud rush of wings,
I am stirred to a strange compassion.

Bells, bells, bells, bells of a steeple ringing!
Wind in the bell-loft ringing!

The walls and the streets of the town
In grey ruins tumbling deep to the surface of the sea
Rest at least in the silver orb of the sun.

Now the deep wine and emerald, vermilion and gold,
An illusion of dream veils the symbol of the symbol,
Puts its seal upon the head, a birthmark to the bone.

Down from the window where they stood in time,

Balanced in man's brief moment for them,
Three apostles, nameless as the thought of them.
Oh, speak to me not of their benignity,
Of the hair that fell, a dusty mist of vivid foam,
Or the wonder of their own eternity!
With arms flung up to roll the world, a pebble
On the palm, the wine-red and the emerald, purple
    and gold...

There is a rocky jut, flung like a disc against
The dull dim roll of sky,
And here, like sad pilgrims, left godless in a moment,
They stood, their hands caught at the neck,
Poised in the fold of each own thought,
Each hand the delicate incantation to a timeless
    span.
He in wine held with the fingers ever at the throat,
He in emerald able to point toward the far horizon;
He in the purple and the gold will bear the star.

But what of the form that stirs across the edge,
Wind whipping up the skirt about the legs?

◆ ◆ ◆

Time was like the snail in his cupolaed house
He admitted the shutters up in the day but down at night
Time was the snail in his cupolaed house.

In the evening when birds gathered on branches
The long even dusk and the hills slender haunches
Reclining and stretching to the edge
In the evening now armed up and gathered to the ledge
Precipitating to the lake and shallow foot the water
Strode the proud man's daughter

Eager eyes eyeing the leaning sky
The one unbranched bird giving it unplaced cry
The turbulent titter of disturbed fish perking and puttering
    water
Neither disturbed nor hindered the proud man's daughter
The rocks and the slim fish of quick water walked beside
    the child
The girl the woman and the rock were nothing meek or
    mild.

Slowly the fox curved out its robin plume
And posing to place out its throat lest it yap to the moon
Clipping the crouched grouse from the brush
Leaping the lean eared hair with its virulent rush
And still the lake remained immune to sound
Though the girl should slant her look to the edge around.

In the evening men may come to water
And men may cool their hands in water

And stare toward the daughter
The proud man's bathing daughter
Round is the hill and round the proud man's daughter.

I am singing as a lover
The birds are perched
O my love how may I tell you
One star has slipped to your hand
O my love how few tears
Do you know how many you demand
I am singing as a lover.

Again I am singing as a lover.
Again the water covers you
I know that my plucking will tell something
I have left the city and have come to this place
O my love how few tears
Do you know I have left my land and my race
Again I am singing as a lover.

The daughter is there alone as she must be
Neither love nor the symbol of the cypress tree
Nor the plucking hands that have for a time remarked

God knows I would have told
The rain would have made me laugh
And running beside the long step as you walked
I might have stood the gaff.
Our only complete moment together
I would have been the subtlest as the lover.

Neither in time nor tide
The things that I wish to you may be implied
Immune to delusion and to me

Inarticulate and mere child without felicity
Willingly give and you be now my guide.

Could I cry out my inarticulate
My head unborn and desolate
My fear quite founded in bleak regret
I walked alone with you and could not keep in step.
I do not mind the rain.

Well it must be as you incline
The rain and restlessness I could not hold
The third cup of coffee to decline
No vestige of the mind could now behold
A devil's luck the business here and now
I question if you glared from your window?

There is simple promise to be put forward.
Let it be as God leaning down to my hand,
Let it be as a pact with men and women,
Let it be with the child I bare of mind and womb
And the lover with his sadness and his wondering,
With his troubled heart that finds small rest,
Who sees his own time in his own way
Yet who never puts upon himself its shabbiness.

I talked of talked of some light caught from some vast
     jungle
Whirled like an idiotic top and woke to find the gibbering
     monkey—
This all in a dream an optical opaqueness.
Always the head, always the head and one vast jungle
Spinning, spinning, spinning, spun.
Dignity, morality, humanity, the sun.
Cleanliness, directness the glint of obtuse truth.
What time is there for spinning worn out thread,
Seeping ape ancestry, knowing the gutter that would be
If one foot had placed one half breadth over.

As the gravity of sky untouched and mute in peace,
Stares with its supreme unity into my eyes
Knowing me hardly the fittest to survive
Yet prodding some man to save me for another day
Even from death and child life swinging there upon one
     hair
Even from now when adult longs and droops to have its
Claims.

What must I swear to these men who have been gentle in
    their way,
Who have given knowing or unknowing few but formal
    shape
What do I offer to the earliest years and home
The force that swept me from my land to be saved from
    dying and the dead?
This is the hour that means the end of paralyzing mind
Knowing so simply as I do the pattern of my days.
On the one hand abstinence the other will.
The hour to be as one among people, as head above animal.
As quiet among noise; as heart against stone.
As intrepid courage against annihilating fear.

The hand moves now and there lies the cracked and crying
    pact.
Father, not of pity or of sweetness,
But one who stirs and yet remains still
Who knows neither of unliving nor of life.
Who meets all objects in their every shape
And yet is edgeless in himself—
What you have spread shall become as something good
Forever in my eyes.

◆ ◆ ◆

There was a devil that slipped
Immaculate wings carried him in
He had bought them the day before
Pretty little goblin with bright new wings
And such a sense of humour
Now? he thought Where? he thought
Just then I stood
I happened to be little too just then
I had my own thoughts and not much more
And he knew things rather well
He carried a good show of sins
In Christmas packages
Paper all covered with goldstars
That stuck on badly and kept coming off
In the wind
Well he saw me and smiled
Here's Luck! Get them as young as you can
That made me smile too
Though I had my own thoughts
And not much time for more

Here's a package to you youngster!
He cried cheerily
A package of stars?
Hell no! there only on the outside
He said
A fine present to keep you busy in the head
Ad infinitum that's what it is
We both laughed at that
And then he shot off to find some more devilment
I was a bit too easy

A package of stars'. he snorted
Good Lord! there's more uncertainty
Inaction and incompleteness
In one sniff of that starry little article
Than there are stars in the blue up there
Or mischiefs in the whole tilt of my head

The Anchorite

I came up to a house on the mountain,
And sat in a room smoking and talking to myself.
There is one devil that goes up in a blue strand;
It is the division that makes me find pain
To hurt myself with, to die upon, to laugh at myself—
It is the terrible face of the wrinkled land.

Fifty years have gone by on every side, I know.
A body tires and dries up and a stamp is made between the
    eyes.
To come upon a tremble of spring here on the mountain,
It is as if an ancient bone gave a low
Girls laugh and I must hold the ugliness still for the
    torment and the sighs.
A witch is more lovely than thought in the mountain rain.

I came up to the house with its winter hemlock,
The sun drilled down into my delight and I spoke:
I have not loved a woman with beautiful feet,
I have stroked myself and leapt but have not found the
    witches' wedlock.
Over the hill I thrust the long strand of smoke;
Here is myself to laugh with and the high-cock's self defeat.

♦ ♦ ♦

There has been more than beginning and end to face.
More than thirst and eventual storm and famine.
There is the strange disharmony of mind and spirit,
Gift of time, family and uncertain heritage.
O and the unhealth of wrong thought, wrong fear—
The dullness arch naiveté and infanthood!
For here lies sin against the simplest law.
Leisure satanic slow and rude despond.
The image worship building in the so called abstract
Mind.
Where channels made never may unscare themselves.
Death acts, freak masks the crimes against direct sym-
metrical law.

What I have not done but seeded in my thought
Felt quivering into half life through my frame
And so attempted to drown in shout and noise
In loud primitive ejaculation and brute moving
Against the logic and the sweetness of my proper brain,
In the truth that we surmise unquestioning to be human
In the beauty that is inherent in our meaning,
These the deeds that have broken tablets and disinherited!

Come, let me grasp the power and the basic law.
Let me know the hand that is of a peculiar coolness,
I give the simple promise of self will of abstinence, all that
is conquering.
That mind be grave and life be adequate.

Poem

I would hold the many sides of love with my two hands,
Knowing, in the hot-cool and overt curve,
That once caught from mind: the inflexible demands
Of time, death attendant upon life, all life to serve,
Foetus light engendered.

When seeing angular children running over bright grass:
Follow the pace, the action and direct child's glance,
Each umbered-innocent and shrilling as they pass.
The shock of sound, the race and stare mark, in the erratic
    advance
Across sub-smooth, neither song nor bleak but vital fact.

The brain, a moon of mother-calm and fertile,
Unfertile in the ultimate of meticulous placement.
Everyman, having figured, having tested, attempts to widen
    to non-sterile.
Only the gently tampered mind conceives of its development
In sweet proportion and, as such, propitious.

It is here and now, the love, the running child, the mind,
Recall divergent sides and selves: that walk,
Move as a pattern under god, expose to the natural loom
    the web of kind.
Love, the child, the thought and to the crest the metaphysic
    hawk,
Finite conscience star-based in the vaster unspecific.

How would we break and how suspend: when dead
In the passionate drowning, the climactic action of our
    living

The fears that hold in the tight seed, the covetous bed?
How to supersede the intolerant tense for more than giving,
The tolerant circle that transcends its shape?

To hold the many sides of love with my two hands;
Neither to condescend the touch nor bitter-brim the hour,
But draw from amphibious tides the underlying concept of
    quiet sands.
Water! Land! Each gull and hawk the height of cerebral
    power.
Recede the body, somewhat. Extend the fragile precepts of
    hieratic soul.

◆ ◆ ◆

Men and women only have meaning as man and woman
The moon is itself and it is lost amongst stars
The days are individual and in the passage
The nights are each sleep but the dreams vary
A repeated action is upon its own feet
We who have spoken there speak here
The word turns and walks away
The timing of independent objects
To live and move and admit their space
And entity and various attitudes of life
All things are cool and in themselves complete.

◆ ◆ ◆

Believe me, my fears are ancient,
And I deal in ancient patterns.
Like the burst into spring, I am defiant
As the shoot, while the bare earth turns;

As the gull from the unpecked shell
Recalls the one act of living,
Totters and breaks pell-mell
With the stark demand for winging;

As the embryo dream moves from the void
Together with the will to be,
Out of the welter and span, denuded,
Into the spawning sea.

In the clear sway of movement,
The contact at various corners,
The mind in the head has content
In spite of conglomerate mourners,

And rejoices to slip over and be convivial;
Yet always there stride strange shapes,
And the gibbers of unenviable
Fears swing like promiscuous apes.

Believe me, I am lapped by fears,
Split and contaminated:
A jungle life out of the jungle peers,
Though the sun gleams unabated.

◆ ◆ ◆

Here where I tamper at the inverted walls of tomorrow;
The gathering of old women about their bagpipe sorrow
In the dry room of their choice,
On each knee a cup, erotic age—virginity in each voice;
The strident tired and cryptic knitting
Clattering on and on while my fingers flitting
Over impregnable surface warm with the friction,
Callous, ice-smooth with the next day's obscurity of action.
Here where I finger, only yesterday having thudded out
With an evil beat that leaped from extremities of doubt
Till even the head thrashed—the pauper skull
Acclaimed itself in every drum the Calaban of dull,
The height of down, the unnumbered telephone operator,
The stammering apologetic politician debater
With blown papers on an evening pier
Once having dreamt the speech and equipoise subordinately
    dear.
Leave the head to its particular swimming,
The hand as fist where it belongs the finger to its skimming.
Walk the path with men and women and consult
The attitudes of little children.
Treat with gravity the statement of the parrot and the hen;
Run with your hands in pockets whistling and listen to
    sharp wisdom
From your own spontaneous play, even from
The clip of your heels under night lamps and on in the dark;
The hieroglyph trees marked thin and bare about the winter
    park.
These are tools of questioning to be met and used anywhere,
To be bumped into like workmen with thin collar high in
    morning air;

Such people mistaken by the careless for the unancestored
Born of reflex, the machine with its virginity of assembled
Parts. Non-life to live birth death and food,
No choice to sense the devil or the good.
Time who pours the terrible mother of fruition,
A brisk director of pageantry, war and balanced inclination;
Narrow in sense, repetitive in ideology and plan,
Endlessly creative in detail, sparing each man
The head to dream, the brief right to turn and lift his hand;
To shout some hate, some gladness and some pain to some
 demand.
About the hill and valley striding-small the moment godhead
Working the rhythm of the race over the races quieted dead.
Gathering time with all the little perceptions abbreviated
Shading their eyes and breathing jerkily in uneven rows of
 the belated,
Each calm clarity hanging its head to forgetfulness
For each drooped man and shame and each too cruel distress.
The panting over the hand loosed from the hair,
The long tempered point implies the touch from wall to air,
The surface fingering of the inexplicable. Desire
Of the infant have pulled one step but being young must
 wait to ascend the next step higher.

♦ ♦ ♦

In the night we peopled evil forests,
Running naked with our hands against our mouths.
And trees hung muted in those evil forests,
Over Druid temples, razing primal tithes.

Now in this sleep we riverrun.
Eye to eye mouth to mouth unspoken,
For rock is flesh and the oval sun
Eye to eye, mouth to mouth, unspoken.

Walls of early smoke the leaves,
Each in an autumn's roisterous trail.
Even the dream a pulse of sheaves
Out of the hoar-mist tanged and frail.

Scaling of the lifting eye on-set;
O and a sigh and the pass of years.
The rod-bent, sea-spliced season met
Only to flay our primordial fears.

A night spent in watching
A night spent in watching
Night
A halfwing of thought lifted
And drifted
Out
Thought in answer to awareness
Of thought in awareness
Of night
She is the sphinx with stretched eyes
And the coiledblue of her hair flies
At the moon
The weight of her lips pressed and pressed
On the heads of the blessed
Halfdead
She speaks and her words are the mumblings
Of the infinite to the jumblings
Of the dead
She is a deepbossomed shecat watching
With green eyes
The sun with green eyes watching the
The night
The dark trees shiver at the paleness
Of the deadawake pressed in frailness
Out
And they grow hushed within themselves

◆ ◆ ◆

Instinct and sleep you are two passages that converge
Two faces that stare and reflect back one vision
The sea and the night both stir their profound surge
Each shouldering on the boundary of their prison.
A man who has raised the inhibited line of off horizon
Will stretch his thought to the beach where two converge.

Now as the man starts up to follow out the shape
That the welding of a dream and touching of a present
Has clipped out and molded of horizon and the cape

Dunes whose sands wash up to meet the sea
And all the slopes aslant and thin lipped blue
Waves with their fists and their shapes drubbing
Evolving dry bubbles at their thin lipped spitting
Immaculated waves wind-flipping.

Run I down to the water and sea run up to me
I am rolled in your uneven turbulence and mind
I'm adulted in your poised pant and pawing
And lightly gulls and birds are cawing
I am bent to the coastline running.

◆ ◆ ◆

Sleep whose hour has come
With fine fingers and lean lid
The end and sum
Of the day passed through

Sleep who walks by the water
And knows the deep
Rather as the woman quizzical her
Mind placed for the leap
That is inevitable at dark

Beds may be banks
Seas may be happier beds
Soldiers that drowse in ranks
With cool earth under their heads
Drowse with a timelessness.

Sleep the sum and end of a day
Calmly the pattern of our instinct
Patters its inconsistent say
And sleep is still retribute.

◆ ◆ ◆

River of light
Bombard the night
Or what have we to say, This is a little thing?
Or shall we sing?

We had built this seed on seed two grains for every
    thousand years
You must not forget us now we bear other seeds.
In long deep rivers of Lethe you may not forget us
Or those you would forget and yet must build upon
All the immutable stone and great earth
All the days that are to night what this is to man
And the shouldering hills through musky hollowed dawns
Precipitate the shadowing sidling flanks of the past
And future on.
We had ancestors high might men with beards that flipped
    in the wind.
A little wind for there were gales to see in the pregnant
Stare they turned along the land.
It is earth they cried earth and the rains came down
And the far plowed fields burst up with a new clear bell of
    green
A very sound rung in the temper of the newborn spring
I think the old men must have turned upon the stars
And whispered in a young world's ear shoving the cracked
    palms
Of their hands against the ground while their fine
White heads caught and held and dropped with each return
    of sun
Each wise thought and half form dream.

Those thoughts without words that made him sing
Those are the hands that cup rust like the tail of a fox in
    Calais
The bodies of half deed half dreamed wavering along the line
Making faint patterns in the caked clay of their brittle bones.
Small incredible as they grow into the stone we build upon.
Now we turn to you great cities and we are dumb with our
    own
Doing.
These were spun of our heads and whether they will be the
    tombs
And the testaments of tomorrow?
Whether they will look with great incorruptible eyes into
    the
Tomorrow? and bear us witness to a better race we do not
    know.

Do we mock ourselves with turret mosques and cupolas
    brittle
Light spattering out the gilt and feathers of a brash pale
    people
Is this a world that sings its own song and ends within it
Or is it at last the flutter and the cry of an eagle startled up
Of all the eyes that drub along the surface will there be one
    catch beyond the the moment
High as the dark that trudges into night, the cities beat
The incalculable pouring of mass streams into the streets
Of the meeting of man and man
Like cool stone poured to the palms of a corrupt shivering
Back to tangle and be lost—the strand of water weed
The old men whispered stars and this is a new world
We were blown a great insoluble riddle by some triton horn
Out of the corridor the twist and curl of soundless seas

An aboriginal tribe of fingering sun bewildered life
Out of the deep dusk spiraling beyond the enigmatic spleen
Only to return only to return through the pale wash of the
Shallow like shoals of minnows spawning down to the tides.
It is for the young to dream their dreams if they have heads.
And for the old and the wise to see what they must see.
These are tremendous steps imponderable strides.
But infinitely small like notes of a piping across the painted
    hills.

◆ ◆ ◆

1

I feel only the desolation of wide water,
Its back a silver dimpling from the sun.
I feel only the thrill far cry of one gull
Reluctantly chasing its shadow on the wave.
Here, like some lost strand of sea-weed
I remain within myself a sad contumely.

2

Mark, mark the ring of bells, the tap of wings!
Mark, mark, my eyes that turn a sad pool up.
For I remember how the yellow sand slipped
Through my fingers and the night drew a tight
Cloak warmly about my yellow sand stained skin.

3

O to what shame toward my own first cause,
I find that like both sea and air I am two things
Crystal and clear and at the other hand sweet mad.

4

There is a boat with perpendicular sails,
White as the heart of the wind.
I would ask where you blew your boat with sail
If I did not know that the seams of you were cracked.

5

How the gulls cover the water, the path to the sun,
How their wings drift and lift them up.
They move as simply as the rise and fall of waves
And I would move as simply as the rise and fall of
    waves!

◆ ◆ ◆

Even the gulls of the cool Atlantic retip the silver foam,
The boats that warn me of the fog warn me of their motion
I have looked for my childhood among pebbles my home
Within the lean cupboards of motherhubbard and clipped
    Albion

A wind whose freshness blows over the Cape to me
Has made me laugh at the memory of a friend whose hair
    is blond
Still we laugh and run our hands over the sea
From the farthest tip of land to the end of the end.

I had so often run down to these shores to stare out
If I took an island for a lover and Atlantic for my sheet
There was no one to tell me that loving across distance
    would turn about
And make the here and now an elsewhere of defeat.

In my twenty first year to have the grubby hand of a slum
Be the small child at my knee knee the glistening chalk
That sails to meet the stationary boat the water sloping as
    it comes
And all the Devon coast of grey and abrupt rock

By gazing across water I have flicked many gulls from my
    eyes
Shuffled small shells and green crabs at my feet
The day is cool the sun bright the piper cries
Shrilly tampering the untouched sand with delicate
    conceit.

Up beyond the height and over the bank I have a friend
How are your winter days and summer actions
There could be little more than a tea cup hour to make us
    comprehend
A mature man's simplicity or grave child's sweet reaction

Of Wings

Where there are wings contrite
White fronds quivering out without time or space
To limit the weightless lift and bend
Air and the sea bubble-hollowed to hold a sliver-wind
Only existent to the white-cup of innumerable dipped wings.
Here let us wander a moment that tears may fall in silence
As the sea-spray flies and dribbles back to sea.
Here let us wander aimlessly remembering also that one tear
Welled down eternity tripped beyond worlds
To form this infinite sea
And yet must we echo that large happiness with little sighs?

Come touch the hand of my loneliness
Slender as fluted-wings against the sky
As the evening wind is the breath of some more hidden shade
Absently poised between air and air
The shallows and the void.

Of plains of sand that spend themselves
Cherished the early moon
Of minute moments in a breath of wind
Drawn deep in the lungs
Of that there is none
Of home that there is none to stretch
Up the whole mad gap inadequacy
Of many things existent and nonexistent
In perhaps the hollow meaning
In this I have the philosophy irrelevance
And yet a fiddlestring bowed on and on
Can only ache with bleak fingering
When I pause what is there to say in words
I can then only see tepidity O river
Mother Mother my heart is like twin infants
Suckling dew out of grass
When there should be roisterous breasts
When there should be cornstalks whacking
Their vivid sweep into the core that barren bares
Tombs tombs more tombs
Mother you have borne the inevitable
Twins of bald conception
Therefore I do not cry more militant in words
I merely say my say as when the day is grey
Of simpering tirades in girls
Of tireless quality of innuendo in the shades
Of things incalculate unquestionable abstruse
Born of the irresolute myself that lies oblique
Cool cool and let there be stars for this irresolute flute

Poem

It is not I who am sleeping in the rock under the wood,
Nor are my limbs congested with cities or the leaves.
I am lifting and dropping night and day with a good grace,
Each after each in their immoderate halves.

I have no memory to inflict unless I may sing to you,
And the weight covering my mouth holds me back.
The valleys will repeat my secret in a few
Wordless blares, or the hunter track

Toward the hollow of the brain that I would not admit;
Being the place of fawns in the angles of the tree,
The child's bound corner, or the limit
The birds must instinctively secrete in flight or be

Swept into the erotic sun or the edgeless tide beneath.
It is not I who am sleeping in the rock or the wedge,
And yet I thrust back the wrinkled earth for breath
And in the dark extend thin wind stalked fingers to extract
    the brittle ledge.

The Coming of Strange People

(Written on the day of Holland's invasion)

So many bodies flat upon the stir of spring.
We know too well the old war chanting,
The intense green fields that have arms
And all that is the day of man in fallow.
Bitter I am at the sky for its coolness—
Head against the earth and this my earth.

Strange people, where are you stepping?
"Men we are, with our beautiful evils pointed.
How lovely are our demons, how silver winged,
The shout of their droppings in our throats!"
Is it hate you have for this world then?
Strange people, would you have less of us?

It is a bewildered age that talks back and forth,
One man's eye to the ground, another to the space.
From here see the valleys and the banners.
The hollow places will hold ruins for a time
Then the sides of the mountains will green and flower;
Even women shall bare trees and know the leaves for
    children.

Poem

The speed of planes was still upon the noon,
The whirling planet stuttered and drew up.
Reaction in all quiet corners tongued its inactivity,
Windows were slammed and men stood circles of eternity.

Words once spoken spoke themselves.
Trees lavished the hour with leaves muttering,
And arms extending scissor-clipped the wind.
Rocks blocked their way, allowed the atom to titter and be
    kind.

Each misplaced was replaced once again;
If tumbling was not known tumbling was admitted;
And you were there alive, awake in your dead places,
A well patient among similar well cases.

◆ ◆ ◆

Ahab the super-monomaniac, the finite creation leaguing it through the torturous underseas of ungod sought all life damned pain chanted imaginings. Ahab the strain of the inexplicable the man fathomed bitterness. We who turn slowly forcing our consciousness to conceive of passivity in land in night in stone. We who are rocked to the bottom of our own inability to dent to stammer or to guide to restrain the slow annihilation of the coast the shift the imperceptible movement of inanimate dissolving all along the line.

On Looking at Left Fields

1
In the old fields the old corn tangles.
Remember, these lands were green;
See how the sleek weed twists and strangles.
There is more here than is seen.

2
Dried leaves like scales over the land
And the slow blink down to winter.
Father of shivering times crazed by each spring's demand
Why would you know your daughter?

3
It is this London they will never know;
Something of must, stale bread and spring,
The fattened dog the thinning child and Rotten Row.
To be born a Londoner, as I, gives meaning to the thing.

◆ ◆ ◆

London sits with her hands cupped
The day has been quiet in spring
Only street calls and the far burr of traffic to disrupt
The gentle sun the sleek grey string
Of pigeons wedged on building tops
A few cocksparrows puffing the crop with dung
Follow the fat flanked mare as she clops
Flips out her hope where the nose bag hung

London sits with her hands cupped
The pigeons splatter pink etched feet
Leaving no mark from the shelved erupt
And time worn weathered street
Up and down the doors shine newly painted
Now a cherry red out of the subtle greys or browns
The brass polished and the steps a sainted
Smooth of well scrubbed white

All the flat front gaze immobile windows blink
Doors press their frames in rows of chaste warm colour
While slim weeds of ivy slink
With a gayer sheen against the duller

London sits with her hands bent
Letting a later light spill into golden pools
All Easter lilies carried home speak of an early lent
Stirring the quieter thought into into the quieter spools
All the spring flagging its way with lily and with daffodils
Till a cool breeze speaks out of some darker street
Clouds shuffle up from restless intrepidity and spill
There their whole river of abundance at her feet

The whole wide clean river
And wrap her in one river of sleet
To her sides in one wet sheet

◆ ◆ ◆

Ilfracomb is a sea town where rocks elbow
The head of the island-once-kingdom,
Beaches slightly sanded and low
Promontories denying the weight of the water—
Here and there gull splattered, weed coloured, some
Stained to an even brittle green and sheen as handled pewter.

An old shape where the thought has not forgotten
The seeming town of going up hills
And there, down to the bottom, errand men,
Several people passing by vined gates,
High slabbed walls. The smell that fills
Salt odor with something more than salt invigorates.

Then know what it is to have sins of the fathers!
To have had childhood once by water
And not to have had the sharp of gleaners
Eyes nor mind to undry the stalk that sucked time dry.
Not to have opened bright blood to the body earth and there
Fed want for good with good. Relieve the emphatic cry.

Sea, the articulated brain of Devon Rock
Jutting as hard bone down the coast.
Years off from sea and the joints of city mock
At what we have gained and shriveled from the age,
Green and the forest with their folk born host
Voiced in the waves reciprocal rage.

Mayflower with so many angling on their eyes
Away from the early home towards the cape,
Flat in their look, their mouths sea dry and bitter sighs

From converging source flapping irresolute sail.
Nowhere they turn can they escape,
Wherever they touch the land draws thin and frail.

Islander and come down to the leaving boat.
It is true we were Empire and now we are dead and Mayflower
Our faces old ballads shaping themselves afloat
And so many bubbles with fish, with wanness and with sleep.
Seeming town now not even village, hill once tower
Wave alive against Devon Rock and a child's inordinate leap

♦ ♦ ♦

Speaking to Exiles—the one Exile.
Memory, two wedged-women,
Sparse hair, New England boned;
Will know you in your bed,
Will find you as you lie wan-faced
Staring towards sand-into-sea and dead.

Count your joints—gather yourself.
You said aloneness was the flute.
Take upon your knee each meaning—
See what your infants are.
How you will shiver alone—alone.
Water is thin spread far.

Exile, the sprung bow turned into splint,
Yet does that make bewilderment the more?
The equivalent of God is now to find him.
It is the return of epic man—
It is the ring of legend dissected—
It is the clock where sands once ran.

On my knees are two hands,
Those hands, these knees are mine.
Under the sun I am articulate,
Laughter and still by the side of my brother.
In what modern ship-thing did I sail?
Unwomb me now my mother!

Speaking to Exiles—the one Exile.
Words are yours and knowing—
In profile smoking blue smoke

At tables or in far rooms,
Grasping to hold this book, that line—
Whether the frantic age declines or looms.

Islands are mothers into sea.
Sons the frail gulls circling;
Circling without settling minds or lives,
Balanced in the wind, unborn, undone.
Now wrung at the breaking there are tears—
Exile, you are unmothered the islands gone.

◆ ◆ ◆

And though it is evening and I am tired,
I watch the lean meticulous architect's hand
Gather and space the all too harsh demand;

As spider with slender entwined knees,
Spun clock-wise by avalanched honey-bees,
Turns to the subtle weaving of a more insidious web.

So much laughter in the head.
So much of the golden apple and the racing,
The sly won game and tricks of placing.

Now the garden and the mental laughter still,
Rejection never given, never made, stands freak upon the
    hill.
Laughter is better quiet, the smile is heard.

Images of spare Madonnas, Mary Magdalen and Christ,
The uneven walk and the garrulous seeking wine bowl;
All loud reflections on the somewhat soul.

Bend the head to the out-cupped hand,
This is an age for shabby forms and contraband,
Life's macabre and every night replete with its defeats.

We are allowed to place one foot before the other,
To know some valley or some slaty sea,
To hear with weary calm that being born to live, we must
    live to be.

There is small love lost in this strained hour,
Youth dropped down has only dreamt the flower.
The dance of death now cries out for the undivulged
    tomorrow.

And though it is evening and I am tired,
I must gather myself to the mountains,
Only to chant that primal unsexed quiet till
Doomsday for my pains.

♦ ♦ ♦

There is a bursting of the pulse of time
That, like some giant thing, seems born anew
And also, like the swift passing of the weighted lime,
Bears on a tune that infinity drew
Again and yet again from her seared pouch—
And built the puny arms of day
Across the feeble rollings of a restless couch.

One might dream, that by lifting the hand to flay
The wanderings of a passing cloud
There would be rebuilt again the whispered dreams
Of man—strong golden hands, straight back, god-like,
    proud—
Sweeping with the wind through bones and streams
Of his own dry salt-sweat and blood.

But no, this bursting of the pulse of time
Is nothing but the leaking of green mud
Eating its way through this grinning pantomime—
To bear the fruit that holds an odor of a future
Carried inch by inch, along the channels of a darkened way,
Screeching all pain and knowledge from the pure
Simplicity of brain to the level of this twisted game we play.

The Steps of Bast

Ugliness must ever have been of woman;
Woman would rather have been the simpler act.
"I am far too logical to fulfill my function," men cried,
And lifting their heads shouted with a logical delight
    toward the sun.

The calm to disassociate fragments of life was here;
The unclean was not admitted and there was light:—
So many hairs plucked from the shining universal beard.
The womb was declared by all, the seditious fertility.

O, great and mighty thought! O, pillar of fire!
Every female is the reincarnation of some cat upon the
    steps of Bast.
Therefore rejoice with the plaintive reeds along the liquid
    Nile,
Be glad that your sides have other shapes and that your
    laughter breaks.

From the fearful weight of stone ape eyes turn in their
    rime.
This is a world directly gutted by numbed birth and death,
Timeless instinct and the fluctuant flame of curiosity.
Life sprang and crept and agonized, from rock and sea and
    vast black loam.

I am the root, the excrement and flowering, my hands are
    the interplay of meaning;
I am dancing upon two earth curved legs about the fire;
I am the animal, savage, god, drinking my first dark bitter
    wine.

The sleep is my sleep, the waking my waking, the taming
 my taming.

The corn is swaying in rich far acres and there is no other
 gold;
The slow oxen have the brazen sounds of low flutes and
 trumpeting;
There are men who sit in the villages with their brains the
 grist of words.
And all this is the growth in the several heads of men.

Come, shoulder your way then out of your varied skin,
Out of your vicious sex-urge and masked prancing.
Shoulder the burden of cities, of thought and of wings.
Have no more of your stamping but demand clean
 circumcision.

Lift your heads to the brink and let them spin.
You who turn always to the sun, the round hung sun,
Leave the moon and its evil ways to women and the
 night,—
Cats that stir on the step and howl their pulsing life-
 watch.

Every tower and every turret undermined by the craft
Of secret invert gods and image worshipping,
Shuddering back against the too loud shout of the evil-
 exorcisers:
Hard men in wide gold surplice airing their warrior chants.

"Yet our hearts would beat with an age old drum,
And the women would hear and come to us from their
 idols and out of their temples."

Spoke the blunt-mouthed men, with the sudden logic of
   beasts
And rising strode off their freedom thrusting behind the
   structure of their cities.

◆ ◆ ◆

And as I came out from the temples and stared
I saw to the left and to the right the fair haired
The sea eyed the rough throated and the slender young
Out of the temples I take breath and count among
The hoard all the resilient sheen of armor and of swords.

My people O my people lift the sea of your eyes
So that I may remember life from the incensed halls
Let me drown in the reflection of your corn gold life
Spare me and lift my soul with the shoot of many glances.

Behind the temple has set and risen in the gazing ones
The smell of incense has given to salt tang as the high sea
    run
Boats drawn high to each strand and companion shore
My sons are waving from four hills like four
Severe eagles with memories that the father has forgotten.

My children O my children how you do sway my children,
For each newborn I feared and hated and wept against the
    wall
I died my face and tears within my hands the palms wore
    thin with wet,
Wept till I at last leant to feel one with old trees and new
    shoots.

My land where my children and my people wait

After man's passion for strange lands grew tired within me
I went to the well that still holds fruit about the desertsea

Jew Amongst Ruins

1

Jew with the Syrian arch suspended about your shoulders,
Cerulean sky quiet in an oriental noon,
The long black shroud of immutable silence
Has drawn to the bone of you.
Your face is the closed door to cities
And in the immobile length of figure the sphinx mounts
In ever changing shifts of sand.

2

What is time to the yellow grains that stir
In momentary plains within your soul?

3

Messiah pauses when the last ache of your loins
Has spent itself between the bowl and bed,
Renouncing in you the easy thought and act
Toward some sad-songed constellation.

4

All things are to be sung in the high sweet head-tones
Of a desert pipe!

5

Walls were only made for weeping, that and the walls of
    flesh
Wailing to the omnipresence of Messiah.

6

O the exquisite curse of loneliness!
What has the more desert-flute of tranquility
Than this shrilling plucking up to the cerulean-blue
Of an oriental noon?

7

Pull back to the shadow Jew, the gates of Syria
Have crumbled out of age.
You live and stand in the tomorrow
And your wings are the eagles bearing many suns.

◆ ◆ ◆

The caves are sad where the archeologists stood
Out of the old brow of the rocks the wrinkles deepen
The trees whisper like grave ancestors and draw the occult
    hood
Over the horizon over the head over the unspoken men.

In museums small bones show their tender stone
The Neanderthal ponderously thinks his fossiled dream
And Egypt in its case admits more weary bone
Draws the great dust from its sleep and tends the
Sleeper's scheme.

Over in Wales are rivers more timeless than the fish
The Black Kelt still chose leathery bark
Motioning the wiry runt to pass the sour dish
Off on the high cracked crag the first pipe peals the dark

Out of the freak chastened valleys in the night
Where the tired life dodges each from his several pride
Up to the gleaming hole where the warm sucks out of sight
And the weak eyed flesh must hide.

The scavenger dog a retribute for past
Suffers the moon to drop with little more than a whine
And the woman pulling her hair burst from the weight at last
And the man stares stark as the pine untouched pine.

The dreadful feat of the hills come to an infant's cry
Animal step of the wolf and the hawk and the fox
Bearing apart the soul trampling moon quiet sky
Burnt to the earliest god deep in the caverned rock.

The rustle of textbooks over the shallow dish of the river
    more timeless than
The powerless pad of leather and the anemic archeologist
Shouting the source of the river more timeless than the
    fish
Collecting bone from the marrow of past and breath of
The fluctuant mist.

◆ ◆ ◆

"Penelope!"
> The listless fingered Odysseus
> Mouthed at the warmed ripe figs
> That bent the twigs.

"Penelope, why does your hair
In one wide weed hang down?
I had thought it love,
A tearful habit watering the seas.
In barren lights the colonnades reflect—
The flat pink steps
Where dogs once licked luciferous wounds
And in the drunken air
The drunker lovers spewed
Where to you wove with transient thread
A dreary pattern of eternal siege
A black ship battered
And sad bones bleached white
With soft whales' sperm
And silvered round with rime.
Pale tears became the threads
To that shroud nuptial gown.
Up the jagged hill through cypress trees
The Ithacan shepherd pipes on thoughtlessly
While here at last I lie
Tangling the beed honey of my locks
And full of wide surmise, Penelope.
The listless fingered Odysseus
Mouthed, smiling at the warmed ripe figs
That bent a burden to the twigs.

Orpheus: Three Eclogues

I

ORPHEUS. CALLIOPE. THE BEASTS.

ORPHEUS

I died, my face and tears within my hands;
The palms wore thin with wet,
Remarked the tideless sea of swaying lands,
And plucked and fluted and could not forget.

CALLIOPE

Young son of Thrace, out-staring stars,
Binding your song to death and sleep,
Rise and inveigle Hades and entangle Mars,
And tug from death your strands of harvest wheat.

ORPHEUS

Old woman, Mother, coming from clean day
Into my unclear and peculiar pain,
O sit as I do, ranting on this clay,
Drown in these tears, drown in my perpendicular rain.

CALLIOPE

What is this lyre? What your unriddled action?
O why this running of distracted sense?
Several objects speak your sorrow and dissatisfaction;
The repercussions of this dying are immense.

ORPHEUS

These arms, Mother, O these arms are empty.
The earth is round; the trees are slopes
Unquestionably full, while I freeze into sterility.

You know the bottom of seas, wells, and streams,
Where will the songs go now and where the hopes?
Must I delight the twisted root and sea-gull's vacant
    screams?
When I stood naked by my wedding-bed Eurydice,
While the snake dipped away its dreadful eye,
I who had danced with innocents so prettily
Drew them from Acheron the wind of Charon's sigh.

CALLIOPE
The virginities of ghosts stand in uncharted quiet;
Speak about beaches and the waves will find their end,
Run back upon impeccable feet into the hollows, let
Mist sink your words where shades will apprehend.

THE BEASTS
We prance along the wind,
We whimper tentatively:
Be careful of dead places.
Be careful of dead places.
Who are wiser than we
That eye the day with primal panic,
Draw near from crags and caverns,
From forests and furred corners?
We therefore whisper tentatively:
Be careful of dead places.

ORPHEUS
What are those tongues that stutter instead of being dead?
Where do I stand alone? In what moment have I not
    deserved the past?
Let me string my lyre with some senescent thread,
To twang the one grave note and breathe at last.

THE BEASTS
We are growing dull with the sound of Orpheus,
He who once sang so prettily through the woman,
    Eurydice;
We are so nearly sleeping, so close to our beginning.
The little child, the tired enchanter,
Must enter the steaming womb;
The son of Calliope must go down to Hades.

II
ORPHEUS. CHARON. THE SHADES.

ORPHEUS
Old Man who punt the Acheron, what is Hades like?
For Night and Day converge so in my mind,
The one's decay and weed and spawn of all that men
    dislike,
The other's light and flourish, strong and somewhat kind,
I am unable to think of direct end or direct beginning:
The weird kernel of the I stands sexless and devoid,
Mere energy that lives from self, unloved, unsinning,
The end of all that living once enjoyed.

CHARON
In sleep we disarrange the day,
Awake we try to give arrangement to that sleep.
There is the Greek who used to play
Upon the ideal image in some upper deep,
There are the miscellaneous thoughts from all the shades
    I bear.
Each object has its ego-center and its strength,
Its ageless light and microcosmic fear:
A nautilus may die yet through the length

Of time and inordinate generation impress a self, basic and
    endurable
The fact cannot be out-faced of being and not being,
Of moving and not moving; that which we know remains
    forever knowable.
The strong are a flavor and a textural feeling;
Theirs is the bravery of the titillating and obscure
To hold themselves abruptly in high air and spin:
The purity of wind and straining sail and unalterably pure,
The span of a man or the inevitable eon,
Finally and roundly sings the Whole in its all-designing
    conscience:
One man awake, the others still below; one man to stir
    and yawn,
To stamp the calm and turbulence of World with delicate
    defiance.

ORPHEUS

Father of this dulled river without source or sea,
Lean mad bat, dangling upon the sharp point of your pole,
I have swept beasts away from death till they would die
    for me,
I could not keep compact the slopes of Eurydice and the
    tender factions of her soul.

THE SHADES

When you have reached your destination,
Found the sharp even avenues, the sound of leaves,
Noises infinitely quieter than pacing insects,
When you have touched upon the end and destiny of grief,
Along those paths neither shining, subtle, void, nor
    tranquil,
You must lean through all your warmed perceptions to
    grasp that shade:

You will know that it possesses hands though you see no hand:
You will know that it is as a woman should be, walking and
    not weak.
Turn abruptly. Do not look about. Do not stare from side to
    side.
We are lonely for your singing, Orpheus. Take back the
    woman Eurydice.

ORPHEUS
Eurydice! Eurydice! Out of the Grave!
This is the smoothed beard of Olympus.

CHARON
Punt, punt over the soundless water,
Sigh, sigh, die in the tideless stream.
Tears of vindictive virgins,
The negators and the castrated of the cities of sleep.

Weep, weep over the dull green liquid.
As you drown I gather you up
Who may never murmur along the bank
Or pluck the crisp blunt reeds.
Punt, punt over the soundless water,
Sigh, sigh, die in the tideless stream.

III
ORPHEUS. EURYDICE. THE SHADES.

ORPHEUS
Each corpse stretched wide dry distending hands
And each skull dreamed an elongating song,
And every heart, an hour-glass of filtered sands,
Heard every grain proclaim the right from wrong.

EURYDICE

I am rocking the world with the ripple of my thighs,
Drenched in ridiculous laughter;
Over the river of woe, away from the valley of exacting
    sighs
Striding toward the upper globe, I follow after.

ORPHEUS

First I became a note from my own breath,
Stopping all sounds but those that rose too high or too low;
Entering the vacant hall I plucked the mute command of
    death,
And all my intuitions were alert to perceive and know.
Pluto cloaked, and glared with lidless eyes,
And every evil mocked and swivelled and returned,
Lifting great sides to feed their virulent sighs,
While through the whole concept of death the leprous
    sperm-whales churn
I, with all my senses straining by,
Ran chanting on to recreate the intolerant vision
That leaped to hound me back with rant and embryo cry
Into a frightful innocence of spawn and automat precision;
The ugliest mouth cracked, and I filled its emptiness;
Briefly I strummed my lyre, and the tired hag sprang
    luminous,
The mass-head of infinity with repercussive weariness,
And I heard from the non-existent dome a murmured,
    Orpheus!

EURYDICE

A few steps now and the past and the immediate will be
    mine;
I will lean myself to the wind and nibble the sensation,
Passionately grasp the oval bowls of wine:

Taste and tamper have precise delight in the minutest tilt
    of inclination.

ORPHEUS

Yes my entering that world is not their dying:
Eurydice, I am fearful of the dead and the unborn.
When you died, I died with you; the rocks and birds and
    beasts came to me whimpering,
And even the Gods upon Olympus were pedantic and
    forlorn.
A little of my soul grew tired and winged:
How do I not know that I am not nursed under the
    bough—asleep?
Old Charon wisely surmised; "Know what is fact and what
    is dreamed."
So much of my search has been a sensual passage through
    the deep.

EURYDICE

Orpheus I shall tell you that I am. I shape! I shape!
Here is the well-placed head, the delicate trace of vein;
Through wrists and breasts whence these tattered drapes
    escape,
I put my hand upon my heart and feel its action once
    again.

ORPHEUS

Be careful of dead places. Be careful of dead places.
They burst on me and stood in painful circles.
Why should I receive more from the dead than from the
    simple graces?
In Hades the very warmth of tears drew taut and dropped
    icicles.

EURYDICE

I am whole. I was dead. It is harvest in delicious Thrace.
Argos has dropped and prompted one kind eye alone to
    stare;
Into my lungs I draw the whole full breathing of a race
Whose mother hand is my delight, whose cries are my
    despair.

ORPHEUS

I am turning, Eurydice, turning...
It is the wonder of a sleeping child that turns upon its
    sleep:
A doubt without discerning,
A shy hand stretched along the edgeless wall where fearful
    shadows weep.

EURYDICE

In my palms lie these two clear efforts of my eyes,
The very essence of this tormented moment.

THE SHADES

O son of Calliope, do not turn upon yourself:
Every hour a new doubt assails the grave.
If you do not turn back, the past will live with you again
And you will be the immediate parent;
Your song will weave each glinting object with its shade.
Even now you slant your eyes and swerve,
Old Charon's listless tune completely fills our ears.

EURYDICE

Orpheus be quick. Be brief. I will bear you a child among
    the dead.
There is no doubt or crying, mind or fact.

Stretch in the reeds beside the Acheron before all hope has
    sped
With formal hope, far from the intent action and the act.

THE SHADES
Birds and beasts, rocks and fish of the sea,
Watch how the lidless pools absorb to themselves
The improbable adventure without a ripple.
Orpheus, springing towards the wonder of the dead
    undead,
Clasped to himself the concave image and the negative,
Drew to his fluting breath the strange distortion
And kissed and kissed again all that contracted in,
That which had sighed wind-wise and rushed back upon
    its end,
Clutching the tideless water, tiring the river reeds,
A chanting tearful lover, impassioned and complaining.
Birds and beasts, rocks and fish of the sea,
Allow us to return to you your living:
Though Hades is kind to those who remember and reclaim
    sleep,
Leave what may be the absolute of death to us, the proper
    dead.

Letters and Prose

Detroit, Michigan
July 1, 1937

Dear Helen,

I am held speechless in the hands of some spirit indefinite and prostrate.

Oh, believe me, the nights slip an endless chain of thought to where the curve of your body and the subtle uplift of the neck and head are pillowed, and I may only dream that perhaps there is a traced loveliness that is your thought, lingering for a moment in the vacuum of a moment's shadow or a moment's life . . . spreading half-toned wistfulness toward those distances that are my walls of space, walls that if not too wept upon, are tears entire and in themselves.

I have nothing to say. If I am a little goat, you are a little ass to think such delightful thoughts . . . and such a terribly dear child. It gives me an indefinitely exaggerated feeling of pleasure to feel a few inches adult, and then, Helen, I don't know what to say, and I'm making a fool of myself. It's so utterly bewildering to know just how to write decently somehow.

I read your book all the way here and found it extremely

interesting. It had more grip and shove in it than I could ever have imagined and some really excellent touches. I suppose you're attacking your newest one now.

I received your poem yesterday, and after the first shock of realising that you were a thing of substance rather than illusion, I felt rather shy, you know, because I felt terribly glad, especially that you wrote, even though I hadn't written you, as of course it was my place to do, because I should have, as I should have. You must have imagined the devil of a time I'd have.

If one could write a letter so: Dear Helen, then just a line drawn across the whiteness of the page, and sign: Love, Joan, I think that would be splendid!

Just for instance, I've written two pages toward the completion of a novel of sorts, because you wanted me to. I think being an excellent stimulus to the imagination at any rate. When I'd sit down and try to write to you and couldn't, I'd draw out a notebook and try to do something for you, as it were. So I've finished two pages, and that's something, I suppose, encouraging if a bit forlorn.

Detroit, Michigan
July 7, 1937

You will then rejoice to know that I have four pages instead of two. You have the ability to just write, but I have all the multifarious demands of creation to battle against, the worst of which is a hideous perfectionist complex that kills everything cold, an unpleasantly clammy hand that jams right down to the center of things. I sit and stare at this demon of mine and try to see which one will terrify the other out of existence, but she has such extremely lovely ears and such extremely wild-wide eyes that I feel I shall have to make some sort of drastic compromise soon. After all, I'm not a completely inhuman monster.

It's more than true that Detroit is rather a lugubrious place to be, but don't worry. Good Lord! I spend my time worrying about your mouldering your summer away in the midst of a stifling New York. Perhaps that's why you keep on slipping into my mind as I write and into "The Hills and the Hollows," not you, but rather a certain essence, so that when I read it over, I always seem to have the pleasant sensation of having touched the warmth of something.

I have not only leaves, but a scattering of birds and rose-bushes and three very tall poplars that are really topping fellows!

Then a family, noted for its weird vague eccentricities and disjointedness in the confines of Detroit, frantically miserable when they bother to think of it, and heaven knows they have more than their share of insurgents—two artists, two inventors and a rushing mother. When mother and I arrive, it rather completes the circle. We couldn't possibly live together, but for the summer, yes. The worst of it is that most of my family seem to have a fundamental laziness, especially the youngsters, and by the end of a day, we are all pretty thoroughly exhausted.

◆ ◆ ◆

Worrying about a violent look of activity in any one direction. But discounting that, it's really quite pleasant. I wrote a sort of poem. I hope it won't annoy you. It seems rather bad 19th-centuryish, though I don't know why.

But, oh, what the devil! and I wish I were the most fabulously wealthy millionaire in the world for one half second so that I might present you with all the exquisite things your so finely developed taste naturally falls upon to give you. Every conceivable lovely thing would compensate for so much. Therefore I had better hurry up, what?

◆ ◆ ◆

Like children we are always gazing out of windows! In all my head there is no new thought. Where is this god who throws the very solar system out of gear for aspirant youth? I believe that is the basis for some stupidity... Our essential centers are a spire of compromise. I shall be neither male nor female. I shall be neither God nor Gamin, neither hot nor cold, neither sun nor rain, but temperate, always temperate.

Some stupidity is built out of this desire for balance. Balance is the whole meaning of existence to me. Without that goal that points a distance pinnacle, I might slug myself to earth forever. Balance is high Buddhistic calm. Temper ourselves to a temperate mood without the tepidity of cowardice!

I know I am serious without people, as I write uncontact to their moods. The concrete physical has always been dreamt into being. Nurtured through the mind with the exception of surprise. Without aggravation. That too can be tossed aside. If one might have periods of utter objectivity to the stars, living on goat's milk and an occasional delectable lettuce leaf, or even a rose seed culled from the intestines of a nightingale!

Why squander our lives in interminable deviations? Why force what it is to be or not until it squeezes by the board! These questions were once answered with pat words, now with an inarticulate shoulder.

I have come to the sudden realisation that I do not actually know this thing myself. How truly does one know if one is a saturate field in sheep's clothing? If you begin to smell on the surface, how much has whored below? Could one conceivably be insanely wicked, and yet be child to oneself? Not that I quite apply these gloomy words to my own nature. Still, there is the question. How do I know that they are not applicable? What proof have I otherwise? All my life I have had thought as vital as the action.

I tread, retread, the paths of ego in that search for myself. Non-self I must finally touch without shivering in light.

Once you asked me to be your friend. I tried to show you the impossibility; for through the years people had liked me and the responsibility of friendship always seemed to clutter inside me in the necessity of response in words. The last years, a talking too much to those I didn't like as a result of the tightened restraint toward those I did. Perhaps to you it may seem ridiculous, but I feel now a free swing leads toward you. I ask absolutely no more than to write to you and someday see you without words, if there still exists that abominality of attitude and self-consciousness. Now the world is made up to me of peoples impersonal, of individuals personal one!

◆ ◆ ◆

The strangest sort of mood has finally collapsed upon me. It is to me not only extraordinary, but most upsetting. I seem to have lost interest in absolutely everything. Of course acting I had already struck rock bottom with. Now I am utterly winded by the fact that I don't care a tinker's dam about reading or writing, seeing people or not going anywhere, or not dreaming, or not. For a while I felt the very powers of Jove, rock and stars and a dash of sun. Always it's been a struggle against something, toward something, never void indifference. What in blazes does one do?

Your life has always been so packed, so relentlessly flung in contact to contact; yet there must have been periods when inaction finally did filter to the roots and make for something wholly alien to all former hopes and conceptions of yourself, utterly off pattern. Not desolate, but smoothly indifferent, but most unsatisfactorily and almost repugnantly grey to all form, all modes that make of life the living.

Character is an outer defense, an inward sensation, dock where ships of varied cargoes fling off the center-tested weight, or should I more justly call it style? Then, character.

That is what has escaped! An incredible idea gave me strength to build upon, if not evenly, at least to build. Now, with no idea, no belief, no heaven-sent blacks and varied light, I can only wonder now into what riddled pocket of the universe I slipped my coin. Hysteria is to me preferable to the pedantic oscillations of a void. I would rather be mad and bad, erratic and incomprehensible, than vulnerably acquiescent to the drab. I am drab, grey fog! Fleeting ego! Comparison of object and relation, was more than human contact, more than pleasure.

If only the instinct that said rightly and for so long its ache for the sea could stir up out of the shallowness some quick irradiance, span the space, eclipse irrelevance of mood! One may cavort with joy, as you, faced with all the traceries that lift the whole, all the wonder of knowledge yet unfound, all the extraordinary breadth and life that moves, all inanimate. Yet one human being in a thousand reaches at your age the Oriental capacity of true realism.

We absorb within the tips of the fingers, the gimlet eye, the eager tongue, the nostrils dragging the pungent and the frail, and then we perceive color too, color through fingers, color through nose, even taste to color, and so we find our

God and soul, not through mathematics and abstract, oh, no, but through so-called physical sensations. That is the Oriental point of view, to see the perfection in the all too trammeled body, which being, therefore is, and therefore has the right to be most roundly.

Detroit, Michigan
August 1937

This morning I woke up with a quick laugh like the sun. A night can only hold it down so long. Then it curves, looming up at the edges and won't rub back in beyond, to show how extraordinarily small one's capacity for unpleasantness is after all. It's been heavy, ponderously so, and to have cluttered with it seemed inexcusable with my great gift for eternally screwing into notes and impositions. We'll let it go.

Today has dropped several weeks out of itself. Of course no conclusion what's to be done is here, and one must be quite polite to the inevitable hereness of today, today, today.

I see you very quietly among cornstalks. There might be the red sky stretching. There might be space. Yes, red, yellow to the brink, up and down, brown crusted. For those things are as Van Gogh swept them, or should one say, scarred the canvas? There's the man. And where is the pen that scrapes its thought so richly, eh? One sees things very brightly against cornstalks, roughly, a bit mangled in the end of summer, and deep, deepest where you spring slipping. For nature paints herself with cool against umber, trill to the wind and the sea, sea to the earth, sun to the universe, we see. Astounding to realise that very infinite existence has centers out, that the artist relates himself forever to the center, that is the life of concentration.

Paint me a scene of slopes and trees, but let there be two

sad-boned horses dropped toward the dark brown and the greens. Give a world of white and snow. I'd henna the clouds or flip off to perdition. For there's no meaning to it. Give me the lake, the woods, the spaces where you stand. The birds are quiet. The sunset back is still and voidless, the lake a half reflection, and the fields melted into the final mists that fill the shadow, and the trees, a drawing, a drawing back diffused, so that one cool colored thing may become essence of themselves. A simple question answered with a smile, perhaps, or perhaps a little dust that throws a star into relief. Who knows? This is what counts now, and the only thing that lasts. The actualities, the people, move, but blurring so swiftly with time, they are as unreliable as last night's fooleries.

The only sphere that one may comprehend and trust so far as may be, even then, is the third-dimensional forms and life you build within yourself, always alive and near the rich growth of your sensitivity to the root of all about you. Your imaginative life is yours, abstract or concrete, a fungi on other thoughts and feelings. Consciously or otherwise, it yet produces a world three-sided and center solid to the world of flux and flow.

◆ ◆ ◆

In a week or so, I and my multifarious near and dear will be making the extremely lovely trek to Ottawa. An uncle has a small natural lake in the Laurentians, fed by one almost infinitesimal stream, a miracle to me how it subsists. The pines swamp the ground in such a bog of pungent clean-smelled needle leaves. Whether you have been in the Laurentian Mountains? They are made of a conglomeration of sudden lakes, trout streams, birch and maple rising from the slopes and gradually fading to the darker wastes of profuse scattered pine. Rather breath-taking. Perhaps the very peak of northern landscape in the sense of typicality.

Strange that you mentioned seeing the northern lights. It was on this very lake that I first saw them several years ago. Gliding across the surface in a feather-light canoe, the black-jade smoothness of the water cutting the shore and then the sudden shivering to life across the sky! Nevertheless, I begrudge you your sea. She undoubtedly makes the lake out to be an insipid sort of chap and this year I miss terribly that deep-life gargantuousness that I was permitted to touch and most momentarily last summer...

New York City
November 1937

Dear Helen,

I had spent the whole afternoon in the park, thinking very little, absorbing generally as much as possible, touching with limitation the thin-wreathed shades of difference in sound, color, smell and people. No idea stirred toward a life. I was not out for idea but conscious sensations, which as I have mentioned before, my intangible gods are gradually opening to me. It is this wide-spread consciousness that they tried by system and fandango to instill at school. School! how many times has my instinct told me what I should do! Things will come, but never by hot-house instillation. Damned waste of precious moments in these years.

When first I thought of the theatre, I had an intuitive feeling that the dance and proper development of the body was the basic and absolute training for an actor. That I believe, for me at least, was so, and that the only school that might have developed without harm; for its keynote is simplicity of fact without the frill of innumerable concentration points. Too,

133

there came a time, before the harm has sped the forefront of my mind when an urge to do Shakespeare was literally forced to existence. I felt without a doubt that through playing the most infinitesimal parts in the plays I should find a footing both mentally and fundamentally that would carry me on. At that moment I would have given my life to do Shakespeare, but no Shakespeare was forthcoming. It was a natural step in color and purpose of development. Thwarted, the first rumblings of disintegration seeped into life.

How abominably delicate the strands of early upgrowth are! Straw falling from the stack, pin pricks in the cloth, each minute ship shivering the tendrils and destroying the compact pattern. What was? What might have been? What is to be? Having to swim out into the sea of far-reaching ignorance, wallowing on the edge of mental limbo, I can only wonder at the ingrained ego that respects with a center warmth at recurrent intervals: "You are to be the very action of your will so to be."

I have not yet been able to succumb to the utter desolation of complete skepticism. That to me would be a hell to which no human being has a right. The skepticism and inevitable laughter reactions of adolescence are all the alive and vital struggles of the individual toward balance rather than unbalance. And here I believe I may say I understand the great and agonizing half-knowledge of America, the ugly twisting of immemorable bodies with vision in the center and in the center wind. This is myself as I live, as I write, with the stupendous dream sitting immobile. When in God's name will it out? To pound one's ass's head against walls, the imperceptible walls reflected in the action, neither will this help.

Neither this nor that, and this I understand in America, in her dance and in her longings.

Where are we going, this world and I, with our rhythms,

and our new-found old themes, and our cities that are dreams in time? Cities, great pools of forgetfulness. Molecule, abstraction. Is this your talked-up reality? No. Here is built up an unreal poverty, an unreal prosperity, streets that have lost the subtle symbolism of the road, buildings all the solemnity of chaos personified. Cities I shall not give up, only their child's futilities. There is too much richness here for the artist, in its people. Here where people are rivered in interminable blocks, wits have been sharpened at the wrong end. What of the rebirth of the city for I would not give up its magic. Here is microscoped the whole humanity, shilly-shallying from filth to wider comprehensions. There is no sterility, no stability in this people, only the resultant atmosphere of a city. A thousand people live blindly, doggedly, for the moment, so give sustenance to this pile of time and solid essence.

One comes away from New York and the living and the quicker dead, the grind your bones to make my bread, and never leaves. And what a completely different world when one recalls the quaintness of old trees well topped, the green and gold the flowers of age-old springs, the name and quietness of old trees, the houses resting, retiring, blending with the country of innumerable parts that lived and shaded out of momentary memory. My eyes carried from the hard iron pens along the zoo, the puddle where the sea-lions nosed the air, back toppling, to the quietness of old trees, the green and gold far out of age old springs.

◆ ◆ ◆

And here I have wandered half the day in Central Park. The feeling of deep time knows no existence here. Yet I was conscious of a distant majesty and God-substance. I glanced up.

The wind was piercing, the sky clear and blue, the sun bare and splendid in its formlessness still brightly held above the buildings. I looked into the cold brilliance of this magnificent openness. Simply I felt the giant benevolence of space, the intangible smoothing of white hands along the world, trying to smooth the wrinkling surface of the earth. The trees dwarfed and bare, the snow in thin patched planes rolling abruptly to an end in each direction, blotting a certain mouse half-tone of shading that I have grown extraordinarily fond of on wintry days for the very pleasure which it gives me to reintensify the dullness again. That is my limitation. I feel always to catch a distant echo in the actuality of things, then to dream it into two-fold reality in the intensification of my mind. That some day my actual contact may be as strong as my heightened dream and my dream beyond the very reach and vision of my instinctive knowledge. And so I die, Horatio!

Park used to mean to me fenced squares of green, the complacent overtop of well spread oak, nor shall I forget the mystery of sheep browsing under the trees in the center of all London town. The linking of park after park, the twining along the muddied Serpentine. Hyde Park and Kensington Gardens and St. James Park, centuries of distance even in oneself, till we may cry this place is the very substance of all time; for here time flies to sleep. And back toppling to the present, I recalled again the day and place. No, the feeling of deep time knows no existence here; yet I was conscious of a nearer majesty and God.

◆ ◆ ◆

There on the long sheen beach the sea and I sat with the fineness of ourselves calm. It was only till the moon drew

out her face. Then we would chase along the waves and I . . .
So now we would sit a bit. A star stepped in and soon the
great white cup of stars was all in place. I drew myself up.
The moon was behind me. A cry dropped from me and I had
turned to meet the sudden face and all the calm white of the
moon, of her grace. The dogs are howling softly across the
marshland. I'd lift my feet on home, but all I can see of my-
self is what has been. I've rippled my thoughts about my
head, and let the cool night prick the dream. But there's no
dead to me, only a touch of sad song, and that all center now
and in the sweet off note that sings up from the very middle
of me.

◆　◆　◆

Bound on both sides by commonplace drab, even the some-
times gaily packed windows become discolored in an inte-
gral strain of mood. Grayness imparting grayness to the
scintillating sky.

Down Fifth Avenue now piston legs stumping out a
whole mile's rhythm. So many people. Then so many legs.
Why is it that I cannot catch the words about me? The into-
nations seem to have missed the sensitivity of ear. Shall I
ever conceivably write the knowledge of these heads and
legs? The inner touch I hold without this key. Word forma-
tion, intonation? As that misses me, so every outward man-
ifestation of man known to me seems to have slithered out
of reach. What actually have I left when I count my years
over and the growth? A dim consciousness of abstract. A
certain baring of the essence, but no plan, no frame to work
upon. All my walls of Jericho squat down at the faintest
thrust . . . dust! How may I find earth, land, for my inarticu-
late song to sprout from? Sounds and colors, words and

suns, grind, grind, grind, as cooped up here. In where I wait, deeper and deeper waiting. Coming, going, in and in. The lover holding only the aspirant soul, forgetting the signposts of that fluted goal.

◆   ◆   ◆

There is a story that comes to me now that has nothing to do with anything. I had been sitting, whirling around the last thought, when the loons were hollow-voiced across the marsh. I think I had it in my mind that it was a woman crooning to her lover. At any rate, there it sounded back and about me, filling the air with such a conglomeration of the tiny changeling shivers that come to the evening.

My odd head had been full of the memory of mud that comes so rich and dark after the heavy rain, of caverns cut so deep to the height of the hill, or perhaps I was thinking only of mountains. When I thought of the soreness of those holes in the good face of the earth, I swore like hell, because I had a mind to. It was my way of wondering. To myself I said: Here's the night spreading her knees so wide I've struck the moon and the first star. That's why I dug the fists so deep in my pockets and whistled that far-off note. There's no swagger here. It's only the lull of the pines that has caught me up in a wide swing. If I didn't whistle sometimes, I think I'd snap off at the heart.

Being here on the bit of a hillock, with the warm marsh land rising flat before me, I can remember that wild black god. Why should I be standing calling down to him, as he sits in me? But there are great things that don't go, and I'd be the last to tell him.

Listen to me then, you face of a moon. If you had a cloud flung to the shoulder, there would be her. There would be who? I'll tell you; it was everything that I'd ever known. It was new worlds of jade rocks where the plumes of scarlet sun-birds mixed their wings. Men were tiny, gouging their hands into the bubble burst of purple grapes. Warm damp smell of flesh pressing along its flanks. The ivory of women swaying over the rocks and through the stream of forests, carrying crowns of spiral fruits on the very splendor of their heads.

I lay flat on my belly, breaking my neck to see this. If I'd looked down, it would have been my own bulge. My eyes bit hard. If I looked down there were bugs and the long flat streaks of snake. All the wonder of a sun and the rot and rot and rot. But even my own rot was good for the trees.

Up there, I was with the fruit shrieking its orange and yellows and orange and reds. I ran around and around the stems with the brightness rolling its color to my mind, with the music bouncing the green and orange, the purple and green. I am myself met in the joy of it, and the bugs and the trees were gone. Over the jadened rocks to the margin, by the margin of the sea. There's where we stood . . .

New York City
December 1937

Dear Helen,

For a month I am free to build out of my insipidities, little dead-awake ghosts, once so inflated that their cheeks gave off a very hell-to-heaven ruddiness. Free to relax and dig under the lack of virility. Free to read, to write. The old chap of the weed-webbed feet plunked back to his mud-puddle. Free to have this month unbound, refaced, and spun on indefinitely, if theatres do no more than ogle bleakly at me from the center of musty corridors, cockpits, cubicles in time. And so I give you the theatre. To me it rather stinks. Murder and murder and murder, and the ghosts and corpses sit, and you sit and smell grows, and flesh goes, and still there are ghosts, so you say Hell! And go to. I have and I want to grin.

You say that you see more than ever before the correlation between one art and another, but I swear to you that though this is true in essence, it does not apply in actuality. Possibly you may be able to give to any art a moment's coloring as you, the artist, stimulated by a sense of development, of form, grasp thoughtfully up. The star that you cup blinks out! Stars and stars and stars, and how many stars to catch? Even sums, they say, are innumerable, or must you have such reality. Spheres, after all, were only placed to reveal the strength of inactuality, of space, of space outspaced. You can fumble with the thought of passing worlds, but passing space never. Let us ask: is space sterile? Has it a reason and a goal? Space is the mother womb, Earth, world, spheroid, the stream of milky way, these are the products of the life quality of space. Nothingness the mother of life-movement. Nothingness the creator of something, meeting that something else, or the same that was, till there is born through airlessness air . . . split from the very groins of space, bubble-bent seeds of growth!

How can we then help but feel infernally complete? We are the veriest seeds of inexplicability. We are the seeds, the earth-seed, coughed up in its insoluble desire to touch. We cut the very surface, dig to her body-swells. To the great womb-mother we twist, aching with the same life-rhythms as earth and animal reflected once. A child that wonderfully bites itself with the first tooth, unconscious of use or relationship between the implement and the part, and bites again. So man-earth and earth erupt, revolt, despise, fear; eternally brutal, eternally running to each other with the hurt. No sooner soothed than hurt again / Never earth hurting earth as man earth and earth man. Sing of the earth, of the mother-space, of the spirit, O man, for you are the dream of earth, and the desire and the life and the growth forever!

And that, my dear friend, is the great new-old fairy tale that the child and the philosopher, the poet and the fool, toy with, and most excruciatingly today. Very nice too that the hobgoblins of the earth, the toads and toadies, may exude their own morsel of expert abstract metaphysics. No one could conceivably say them nay. For who is to deny, to repudiate, a thing built upon words, intuition and nothingness!

Once upon a time a world believed in the little-folk and the wonders that were wonders beyond all wonders. There was a seething under the land of dragons and the cracks of the earth bubbled up the witches' brew and the fine strangling stench of brimstone. Magicians slunk to the sullen up-point beards of forest as the early sun snapped back in place, hunching between brambles and the whispering that was morose and all of a kind in the leaves and the branches and the hidden stir. Never was the world more alive than when men's minds could change the shadow of a night-bird's wing against the moon into a living contumely of death and witch-backed brooms, and what horrified them in themselves jittered in black-magic and chattered from here to John o' Groat's.

There was the silver magic too, and the wine magic of the harvest moon from deepness to a shivering delicacy. And the deepness was Pan and the nakedness, the plop of grape pulp and the crimson stream spilt, spilling down till the belly alone protrudes, a white-silver drum. The rest is shadow, Dionysius, for your pipes are sharp and trilip a gay fandango.

Now the lift is melancholy, O God! what space is this melancholy loneliness? Desert, Arabia, Sphynx, the sands dry to your lips! Incorrigible infinity. Why must all vastness veil its eyes, as the Sphynx, the Pan, the Woman? Startled, the troll kneads his thighs, a perplexed quality in each heavy-rolling skull. Elf, the fay, the little people of the slattern hills, wood streams, not even the twig, the protruding whisper of some perched night-cat, are infallible against their desire to trip to the tip of infinitesimal dangers. A world of men-imaginings brought to a reality. Seeing himself reflected from giant to atom, from god to devil, in a night. The old tale of a people this, and now the new tale, as the old Indian Vedanta belief is said to be: "The doctrine of the self and not-self...a metaphysics of intuition."

The desire to a universal meaning is a pat phrase. To charge again and again the balance-house of instinctivism and tear it to some semblance of comprehensive outer form. To what end?

I remember saying one thing to you: if you would be the artist, you must have the firm reality of a consciousness, consciousness in the never-ending, the great wideness that one must blend withal. There is some gigantic gravity center, I believe, where things may not be considered in scientific formulae, based upon no angles, forms and substances, lines, figures. Nothing to do with space as we know it. It is the composite absolute of nothing. Now to use this certain reality correctly and put it to some purpose. Concentrating too much on the distant hills, one may forget the life, the color and the necessity of the moment.

❖ ❖ ❖

So far I have read two books and feel a thousand times relaxed, as if I had actually time to live again. Time seemed to grow into a drum-beat sounding in my mind till all I could hear was lazy, lazy, work, work, work! Finally the damned words lost all God-given meaning to me and I could only sit and pray for some sort of rejuvenation out of chaos. Now I feel that I may try and piece together...develop a wholeness and a purpose out of fringed ideas that seem so small and run tangent to each other.

I read *Eyeless in Gaza* last week and found it both interesting and quite stimulating. Faults it undoubtedly has. It was not completely rounded and the method of writing, startling and well handled, though impossible to be always lucid in contact of chapter to chapter. Nevertheless the man has insight into both sensuous and intellectual experience that proves it most worth-while reading. I will admit I had some emotional jolts now and then, and though I have heard considerable complaint against the morals of the thing, there was actually nothing put down that the average person does not know and know well. The idea and inner growth of Huxley himself have sprung uppermost to mind. The morbidities, of course, I shall not forget, nor the feeling of colors in passages, nor the vivid reality of characters. Yet with all this, it is a young book, almost I might say an adolescent book.

Also F. Yeats-Brown's *Lancer at Large*. I had read the review some little time ago and had mentally tabulated it as a must to be. After reading *Gaza*, it seemed to flow right into the established frame of mind, of thought. Autobiographical it is, as you probably know, about the author in search of a "guru", or teacher, to clarify, to guide him through the remaining years of his life. Completely sincere, extremely logical in many points, interesting to me even in details of political and sensational exposé, which are simple and matter of fact. None of the sensationalism of *Mother India*. The experimentation under Indian leadership in some parts of the country is, it seems to me, most practical, combining the machine with the consciousness of physical and spiritual development. Properly applied, what a miracle of possibilities there is in the modern life and the modern machine!

Democracy today is incongruous, democracy as we know it; for where are your schools of higher development and deeper perceptive expansion? You expect to build gods out of the gutter, and the man that rules or voices any breed of dominant opinion must be at least the rudimentary stuff of gods. The moment the higher intelligence is anticipated, there should be an almost automatic placement of person and mind in channels of super-thought, super-feeling. India has and is, in a few communities under the direction of men with the finest blood of the past and sensitivity in mind and perception into life embodied in their whole make-up . . . India has and is showing the western world the perfection of a balance, showing them what is so absolutely obvious that it seemingly cannot be seen. Hopelessly masculine, this world. India is wise. She remains Mother India.

She remembers that she is the mother of religion in the past to our future. The man when he is momentarily young I have noticed, and we all become infants at moments in our lives, literally drools in swaddling clothes, helpless, inept. He eats up the moment as he eats beefsteak, flushed, with gravy on the chin; if it is a woman, an emotion stirs him to the quick. The woman becoming child is six years old. Relying on no one, she stands on a rock with myriad shells rose-pink scrambled at her feet. The sky is the very biggest you can imagine. That is the woman-child and that is, I believe, why she closes her eyes and closes them down / I think I have a feeling that in some way Huxley and Yeats-Brown have met. At least, it is perfectly conceivable, both being in England, both writers.

This is probably the most ridiculous letter I ever wrote,

but as you said you would like to be a sort of safety valve and I have no private life to reveal that you do not know, and I'm indifferently afraid a few other people, it must be thus and so.

It is Christmas. I wish I might send you something. Some day I shall, as I shall many things if it is so written. If not, truly I will not, for that is as inevitable as that water with a surface reflects and blows.

I am trying my devilish hardest to leave New York after Christmas. Somewhere near the sea. I think the sea would be 'whelming during the winter, such blue in the sun, such ice-green in the dusk!

Well, best wishes for the season. It is splendid that you are so unalone, mein guru!

LETTER TO HER MOTHER, PEGGY MURRAY

September 23, 1940

The house will have two radiators when you return, one in the big window, another near your instrument. They are not able to build pipes in the walls of these old houses, so we have two beauties in the corners of the room. Today, after my Relief work, I tried to get the plaster off the floors and to civilize the house. As the bed where I sleep must be out because of the large pipe there, I thought that I would move the couch to its place and my bed to its place. A wise move, for now people will want to sit on it instead of struggling with cushions and wearing edges down. I have a desire to get rid of the pictures up now. I am quite through with abstraction and surrealism. I have sucked what I needed out of it. Perhaps the walls simply plain would be pleasant. I am getting rid of numerous of our books. Rather to have a few that we must and will read, than several by vague authors, or not too good ones by the best. This book by Wyndham Lewis has taught me a tremendous lot about things that I had never thought of before. He believes that such books as *Peter Pan* and *Winnie the Pooh* have given the Anglo-Saxon people a tremendous holding back and utter sentimentality toward childhood. I see clearly the insidiousness of it now. I think some of his feeling is personal in the book, but he strikes truth and deep truth I believe. *The Doom of Youth* is the title.

I feel so much less the weakness of not having strength to see life as is and that terrible pulling down I had. Of course I have growing pains, which I am not too fond of, but in the calm reading and writing moments I feel them to be so clearly and unfingeredly my own.

It is a lovely night tonight, and people and footsteps pass by continuously. I listened to a corner speaker on his box for a moment and bought a supply for my need. I have to get polish, Lux, and the floors will have to be redone. Troy said that they would do them as soon as all is over. Whenever that may be! Please don't expect them to paint or do anything. L. says we might as well relax and be happy that he doesn't switch the rent up a scale for putting in the heat. I believe the best thing is to do it ourselves—or myself. The floors in the kitchen and the shelves ...

I may ask Auden for crits because our struggles are in many ways alike and we are more of an age. As a creative artist he has not only talked but led. He has used his knowledge. Because I have several weaknesses, my battle is an intense and lonely one, and I must not splash it over onto others. I am even glad for this struggle, for it makes a clear goal so alive for me. If the people I have known so far have made me wish to hide from them, then I am through with those people and that world. Don't tell me that I should go out and mix and should be dancing, etc. If I look about me with a thoughtful eye and see no one, why, I don't at all mind waiting. It only makes what might be a productive time a bothersome one. I should be out! I shouldn't be so serious, etc. I think complexes are formed through it. If I don't wish to see people, why shouldn't I be able to say to myself that I don't want—admit it—and therefore not? After all, how many people are anything but so selfish as to drain on you?

It has always been that expectation of those things about that put too much weight down upon me. As my life has fashioned me, so I must use it. If I wish to be grave, serious, why should I be afraid of it? After all, most people do not realise the divisions in themselves and on every hand. This is not an age for attempted laughter. A smile, perhaps, but not noise and loud sound. The whole battle of life is to see how grave it is and how thoughtful one should be about it. The humors and vilenesses are stems from the center shoot of clear widening perception that we must all find. Never let yourself be the little clown for others. They only take it as a moment's dope and you lose something finer in dancing to their infant minds. There is nothing more beautiful than a person who looks levelly and quietly in your face. A smile or a frown from that person means so much more. Good heavens! I don't know why I preach so much!

LETTERS TO W. H. AUDEN

Undated

Dear Mr. Wystan Auden,

I did not know whether you meant to send the manuscript back at all. I stayed awake in startled surprise over its return and criticism for a night and so we are in this respect at least of one piece. I am glad that you seemed to like the Eclogue to be, as you have given something of strength to a thousand years' lost ego. Now I walk about with a careful pride, saying to myself this or that fellow has not done something or other to make him feel as splendid as I do.

I was up to a rather off pursuit this last month and a half. I remember trying to tell you about it last season, and you said, Oh, boy scout stuff! And left me slightly nonplussed. I shall tell you now. I went out in dungarees and a small pack on my back and covered a scattering of New England states at a tangent. To me this breaking away and arriving at lands' end is a source of wide-eyed surprise. To be anywhere is quite unbelievable. How hard I try to grasp the Vermont hills or Cape Cod dunes. It is not that I am one of your swooning nature worshipers. God knows how often a hill or a clear night sky and I have glared back at each other. I go out quite like some small shabby Quixote to do battle. I will not admit nor yet deny the stretches of and complications on every hand. Sometimes I frighten the sea. This time, lead, and flattened smooth as a dull sun, it frightened me intolerably. In my belt I carried a small but keen Finnish knife with a reindeer bone handle, my fetish companion, I had a touch of pelt on the scabbard, which I smoothed down and put beside my head wherever the evening and my journeyings had brought me. It gave me much more strength than the various friends I would have to visit all along the way. It is always a meeting and escaping. You see I never know what to say to people. That is because I have been mentally asleep for such an endless time. Thank heavens that's over. I'd breathe and get off to a six o'clock start. Here and there I took mental notes of outlines such as hill shape against the horizon so that some day the portentous simplicity and space would slip into writing. That I like to do. Translate broadly, press down over and over again this is what you must reach. These lines have the loveliness of gulls' wings spread, and that is not far from exact word phrase or subtly pointed thought. These come much more vitally alive in writing to you. The wall breaks down that always bars my direct contact with the object.

I never am a part of the thing till this moment. It is a bit worrying that I so rarely feel even a momentary belonging. I suppose I have to dwindle it down to the palm of my hand. I would indeed rather spread myself out to its height and length.

I am so very glad that you were not held in the city for the summer. Mother mentioned that your one plan had fallen through. I was at Stockbridge for the Bach program and around and about your part of the world off and on.

There is one thing before I close. I should like to thank you for the completely thoughtful way in which you handled my thoughtless behavior at the New School. Perhaps I should not have brought it up. I cannot yet follow the whole motif, I felt a form of general revolt as much mentally as in any other respect. A dash of exhibitionism too I would not doubt.

c/o Mr. E Newton
Rockledge Road
Saranac Lake, N.Y.
June 9, 1941

Dear Wystan Auden,

I have been trying extremely hard to hit something of the spot in myself that produced the Eclogues. An idea that had been in my mind for the last several years came to me. The dance in this country, I believe, tends toward theatre. The spirit of experimentation has not left the field and the people are not over balanced with a desire to gain more than they may need financially. They have all the will the strength and knowledge without the absolute tradition. Add the word and the frankly lyrical or imaginative frame to this urge for movement and you would have a compact good verse theatre. The American dance is, consciously or unconsciously, struggling toward a verbal articulation. First they realized form in space then act in space. They claimed the awkward, the ugly, the unafraid and the frankly shrill. But the heritage of our age, form in space, act in space, has very little more along the line of evoluting the human whole than the questioning of tears without the tear, of laughter without laughter. The fact finding fact dodging contradiction of the day is manifold in the dance as with the other arts. We press so far back for solidity that our creation stems from stone and the inanimate and technical. I think perhaps our age might be linked more closely to the stone age than the ice age, so far as we are concerned for grey masses of hard men in their mood and oneness reflect some vast and fundamentally inanimate stone rite. It seems to me that we have not been looking for the beginning of men but the beginning of things. We are still using gestures rather than words. If therefore the American dance has discovered much of its technical root and wishes to move on it is the place of the modern poet to give it its vocabulary as soon as possible.

I did not agree with the statement you made once, that dance was adolescent. It is simply a selection of movements. Movements could be or come from anything old young or timeless. As to not liking Martha Graham, well that is a matter of need I suppose. What ever she may not be she is theatre. She is pioneering into the drama and with good material at hand would do, and I do hope I am not touching too sensitive a spot, a better job than Columbia. If nothing else she knows how to work and is not wholly without the courage to adventure.

My young Unemployed Architect has been on my mind for a very long time. I am not too keen to have much movement beyond the moments mentioned. I do see how it could be done and if I am unable to handle it yet, I know that it must come.

If only I don't disappoint you with this brief touch I am sending! A decent Epithalamium may be forth coming during the later scenes of the play or, perhaps, it is something that I must wait for connected rather more closely to direct experience.

We have taken the top floor of a large and solidly home for the summer and, if you are not drafted as yet, I would so very much like to have you visit us here. I think that you and Benjamin Britten would have done an absolutely magnificent Paul Bunyan amongst the heights of this hinterland. It is something of his land you know, not far from the border line of Quebec. What is so very much to my taste is the underlying strength and then the almost aching delicacy of the birch trees which are everywhere about. Also the fact that one does not lose dimension even in the valleys. I have felt, wandering about the Green Mountain, a terrible irrelevancy but here I stand staring out beyond Rockledge and feel something expanded even in my own small size. One is not pushed away or misplaced and that is all to the good at the moment.

Hoping to see you very soon

P.S.

I did not want to mention it to you but, though I phoned and sent my new address I have not heard from Decision.

I think July would be a very good time if you are free then as the mountains a most marvelously cool at a time when the rest of the land is not. Would you have time to drop me a card so that I might know?

LETTER TO BARONESS

Rockledge
Saranac Lake, NY
July 19,1941

Dear Baroness,

I believe you will be continuing your trip at this time. I spent the week planned recuperating at the Black Mountain Farm. Robert Flaherty left New York for a brief three days and brought his new film to show to a picked few. I had invited Mother and other friends and though they were late, there was a most pleasant gathering afterward. If I had been at all sure of the date of the picture showing it would have been an excellent opportunity to see you both again and for you to meet this remarkable man. I had mentioned to you that Robert Flaherty was practically the father of documentary films, I believe. The picture was shown on Monday (July 14th) and two days later Mother and I returned to our spot. Three days later I have felt both brave and grim enough to write various letters.

I do feel as inarticulate as I should be in reality. I think I shall tell you of the latest thing I am working on. No matter what may happen, I always feel that I may point to my work or schemes of work as being myself. The actions I make in life are either negligible or somehow revolt. If I am allowed to grow at all, it is one line, I believe I am growing in this line in spite of myself. I did tell you that I was writing a dance drama in verse with the hopes that Martha Graham would be interested in it. It is really terribly hard to handle as I am putting questions to myself as well as plot and leaving it to the pure spirit of adventure and to the hope that somewhere in the sub-mind there is a certain order of higher and lower experience that will give it its cue and stimulus. There is the fresh imagination and understanding. I may hit directly to the core of the intellectual intuitive. One almost has to forget that others have thought before one so that the essentials may be alive and not inhibited by the second- or third-hand reaction generally exhaled. The mind of an Unemployed or universal Architect epitomized in the desire to recreate what is desolated, to rebuild; the fact that the spirit exists beside every terrible destruction; that the sensitive but inarticulate line is being put upon innumerable plans while all is in shambles. The characters are of course symbolic. The jungle that the whole thing may or may not pull through is pretty nerve-wracking. But as I have mentioned, I ask myself the question and the rest is inordinate adventure.

I will give you a sketch for the first three scenes. There is the ordinary man. There is the architect. The chorus and the leader of the Five Women. The Architect never speaks at any time during the play, though he may move. The Chorus of Five Women are both his various sides and themselves and the expounders of the principles of building. The Man is the embittered man of action and experience [...]

I am what might be termed an irreverent reader a termite denting thinly at so many surfaces. Books and I are spiritually intimate we may know of each other's existence even speak of it but any absolute contact any force that the meeting of this mind with that to build sound mental structure seems to have so far slipped by the board. The height the shelves the dust rows of even covers the titles and the things behind the titles interminable as they are fill the head with various mirages across deserts. It is balance and perception deliberation and architectural shape flung here like so many seas about the brain. I shall give and I shall give. That these are the distillations of epic moods and men and all that mean means can be reached by a mere hand stretched out is true but that a thousand generations must be chosen from and that each concept if fruitful in some dissimilar way is apt to form a psychosis a mental aberration. My time their time his time. One is startled into a nibbling neurosis and God knows the well-evolved mind should never recourse to such a disease. It is the little knowledge of the little man. Instead of the hobgoblin today the mental peasant grubbing close to the ground has his own form of illiteracy. So the comparatively decent average middle brain man falls back to a fear degeneracy of the intellect. It may be time and tide. He believes his world rhythmed down to his own measure should be had. He waits for time to draw its limit and allow him certain hours where with grave self-satisfaction he may brood man's history back and forth. At last taste the pages of this book that thought silver-plattered to him on the space of a timeless moment. This is no wrong dream but one dallied with so much that all is eaten and gone past in it. I have read books various kinds and most unsystematically. I have worried whole eons by in worrying on this lack of system. And I believe there is absolutely no limit to the span this breed of activity in the head can take up for a lifetime.

If it is true that the action thought and so on of early years is the root of the future building it might be wise to try to externalize my memory of first reading. In some way cudgel it out for I seem quite unable to recall the path in its unevenness. Dickens the first, and *Oliver Twist* read to me at the age of three. The mood the taste and the shape of characters clung quite clearly to me. More than anything the fact of the mother dying had its effect. I remember at this period an intense fear of death of a kind a something black and whirling into void. Dickens with Ibsen is probably the only author I have completely covered. It is a strange thing that as a child one may be so conscious of a quality of dust of angles in figures of weirdness and dryness that gradually goes. For example Mother has always had a few editions of De Maupassant and Balzac about and always I used to attempt to read these books often having to run out into the open so filled I was with this strange choking dryness. Now to pick up a De Maupassant is a refreshing thing to me. Air and space possess the sentences and the wit and direct sensuousness of the man with his compactness of narrative hold nothing of that unbreathingness for me. This is also true of Hardy and Anatole France.

The second of the early memories of reading was *The*

Little White Bird of J. M. Barrie. This was a great tragedy too in the fact that the window was barred and a strange child in the bed. The poignancy of lost mothers and lost children and the sadness in the inevitable wandering of lost things grew quite early with me and therefore these two books read at such an age are possible to recall now with something of the emotion felt at the time.

Nothing of great importance for a period and then the usual period of Andrew Lang books of Hans Christian Andersen and the Grimm Brothers. Greek legends never that I can recall held me as tales of other lands did. There were the usual delights of adventure and pirate stories Poe and Irving and Hawthorne. English Annuals—the Chum Books preferably historical tales by Conan Doyle and Fenimore Cooper a period swarming with woodlore and Indians then with a suddenly courageous leap at 13 into Dostoevsky with *Crime and Punishment* and with it all a steady undercurrent of Dickens. My taste in poetry was slow and unoriginal tinged with a form of revolt which was slightly overcome through Scott's "Lady of the Lake" delightfully easy for me to grasp and filled with the Scottish background that I always felt such intimate belonging to. Stevenson in some phases held me now. *Treasure Island* and through several of his more adventurous books. Out of this *Crime and Punishment* lingering like an erratic shadow with me for an interminable length then *Anna Karenina* a brief counteract of Charles Lamb whose *Essays* pleased and flavored my mind towards recovery. But the finger points on down the line, average and without too clear a perception beyond the texture and the mood. At fifteen the theatre came up to me and I swallowed biography after biography of its every phase. And from this time I came away with a deep admiration for the works of Gordon Craig. Plays I read to the full, and mostly of the 19th Century. Ibsen from stem to stern

Strindberg and the Scandinavians complete. Hauptmann Wedekind Maeterlinck, Shaw an interminable list. Can I remember one? An abrupt away from the theatre, and the field missed began to be slightly covered. The *Odyssey* at last. *Oxford Book of Greek Verse*. Milton. A dabbling into nature study with Mr. Hudson, and various essays by Pound Tate Eliot Yeats Colum. A slight and late period of the Edith Sitwell and early Yeats with his plays and poetry of A. E. Housman T. S. a moment running over of Hardy and with that Mr. J. Cowper Powys and brothers' books and essays. A strange glimpse into the water babies and its philosophy. Thomas Mann. Goethe. Irish ballads Scottish legends but then there must be a back-wash somewhere in the head of endless books now dissolved and absorbed for the better or the worse. But so much of touching and tangling so much of indiscipline. What sound structure would possibly formulate from these irrelevant small turrets heaped shapelessly one upon another with only the thread of a self felt strand balancing out the fragile spanning.

Drafts, Fragments, and Poems

A Poem

Britannica. Thank God, we still play Beethoven and Bach beautifully. That is one step in our maturity.

Liberty. If this war should be won what is the thing you as a woman shall do?

Britannica. I have found that like most things physically set back I have insidiously crept into fields I do not understand. I have become erotic or dull and have given very little direct strength. The building up of civilization forces equality. Perhaps in the far stars the whole point of our world is to alleviate the child bed. If you handle what small freedom you now possess as heretofore you will become unbearable and lose everything. More and more I shall try therefore to become self sufficient. Not to take the position of the male unless necessary, but in my home. I shall not depend on my husband more than necessary nor on my children for they soon will wish to break. These are all good duties and happy ones but not clinging and embittered ones. A great healthiness must come. Sound mind and sensitivity to the pleasure of simply living.

Liberty. A well-proportioned world I'd say.

Britannica. Thank God again we still have the courage to plan for better things. We so inevitably disappoint ourselves and yet a sudden sun in one morning makes us grasp our hopes and promises again and again. I wonder if Hitler knows the dark and light that goes on in even the least men at times.

Liberty. I should imagine him to have the mind of a nasty small boy. Bully Boy and God.

Britannica. In the end and the beginning it is ourselves we are struggling for. Though we were inert we did our job for gain. Should we know the wheedling voice that chirps us to election is out for every shilling? Even the butcher knows and sneers at that and says he's a clever devil. From top to bottom up and down the cad has had his day.

Liberty. I wonder when the good one strikes the top?

Britannica. That's for you and I to say and do something with sleeves pulled up and thought clear in our minds.

Liberty. A woman think? O dear no!

Britannica. Some women think even now. Too few. Some men think. Even now and too few I say again.

Sterility

Lift up your feathered wings
To let free the heavy stench of sleep.
There was a night when women's breasts
Hung heaped above my sagging mouth,
And dripped their pure sensuousness like juice
Along the darkness of the halls of night—
Or again, some male-thing pressed against my side
'Till I leapt madly straight through reality to dawn.
Yes, but now even those are fading—
Those things that left one panting
In their smooth voluptuousness.
Even too, the flashes of beauty in the intricate
Catacombs of sleep have wandered,
And I am only left with the weight of ghosts,
And the gray things that foul the mouth
And exude the monotonous wailing of the tombs.

Now fellow caught upon the limb
Rest the whole body at an angle
Fingers through your hair do comb
In a pretty mess of tangle.
Hell's not worse than things you've done
There's no wickeder than most
Went from mother on the run
Free lad now an evil son.

Fathers off where pubbers go
City streets and queery women
We're a bad lot in the know
Father son and stranger men
You'll look high and you'll look long
Through the glimmer of a city
If there's all and plenty wrong
It's in queery woman song.

Fellow hat upon the head
Life has made you what you please
Dreaming of a mother dead
Coffined now an ugly freeze.
Grinned at life its sucking pain
Ran from life and up a tree
Things that fuddle all the brain
No worse lad than in the main.

Dawn

Softly moon sips at the glow of rosy dawn,
Shadows purple tinted streak the sky,
Clouds droop thickly on night's bosom—then are gone;
Across the shivering lake the moonbeams lie.

Beauty raises her mobile cheek on high,
Her beauty mark, a shimmering silver star.
The crimson eagle drops its spiral cry—
And soars above the sun's first golden bar!

Things whirl to life across the blue;
Giant oaks climb up the hills of time
Down-bent 'neath clouds of heavy dew;
And so—through arches of the world,
Pass quietly on.

◆ ◆ ◆

In act and in power their people grew sterner,
The homes which were theirs were all left.
Raising their spears they walked to the high road.
They sometimes stopped to gather flowers along the way.

To the palace they cried, to the palace,
And knew the palace to be closed in their hearts forever.
One man dropped. They did not care to soften and passed on.
Lifting himself he attempted to follow, wept against his end

Having taken these mighty roads they found them long,
And rested more often against hedges.
Each time trembling onto their feet they recalled the palace
Which was bandage to them and which they hated.

Song

Let it be said at the wisp of dawn,
That the sigh of Great Pan was the smile of a faun.
That the smile of a faun was the dance to his feet,
With the twinkle of hooves where the old hills meet
O, the leap and the twist and the trilip tril-lil
And an up from the valley and over the hill.

Down from the slopes and up to the sky
Gentle fall leafing russet and dry.
Caught in the silk flank touching slight horns
Dance of the earth thing season that mourns.
O, the leap and the twist and the trilip tril-lil
And an up from the valley and over the hill.

Man listen the moan in the trees and the air,
The smell of the earth mold and musk of the lair,
The tear of the look and the whistle sweet thrush
The patter of hooves in the berry ripe brush
Know it's them dancing and sing as they go with a trilip
    tril-lil
And an up from the valley and over the hill.

Song

Somewhere lies a silvered land
Built of one webbed star,
Around it burns the sullen sand
One deep glowing scar.

Here mad-men pick lute strings
And hang-jowled hounds do howl.
One mammoth python gleefully sings
And every song is foul.

Above the sky hangs low with dew,
The waves lap on the shore.
Quick flits the scarlet cockatoo
Across the sea-green floor.

＊　＊　＊

It was a dull silk day
In wish a delicate cantata
Scratched diminuendo.
Mirabelle meandered in the room
Her hair was caught a knot
Where it might have cast
A purple cascade to her knees
Her eyes spun up to scarlet
Petticoats
But Mirabelle a pet
Remained the winter through
A pert pink child
A rosy cheeked young Jew.

It was poppycock he said
To expect the weather to change
When Christmas trees were tinseling
Like anything
There were seventy thousand children
There to here the flat remark.
Each one blew a bubble
Without the least compunction
Whatsoever.
It's this very young generation
He murmured disconsolately
Oranges as round and ripe to burst
Candy cane and sepia balls
Pretty petalled pompoms peach immersed.

Mirabelle said I don't believe in God
Turned and sucked a stick

A green and white striped stick
And rubbed her hands
On anything she could touch
His high silk hat for instance.
It was only a moment
Before she was ogling herself
Surreptitiously in the glass
O do you mind awfully if I twist
Myself up like a jackknife
My grandmother prefers whist.

My god where do they find the brats
The lights sparkle sienna purple yellow
Just like the autumn bursts
Foam of leaves spattering dusk
But the cantata plucks plumes
Of pale staccata
Brims airily a damp sleet snow
Flaked and fluctuant
Sterile with moon she waves her hair
Down in wing of petulant purple
Portly bilious old maids
Mirabelle how she laughs at gregarious Myrtle.

◆ ◆ ◆

Now whether the dead are here?
The ochre hound, the Indian,
Somnambulant in every thin strung step
The crackle of ancient bones
The fine moss of old heads.
I listen, lean to the ground,
In autumn I finger the skeleton leaves
The dry brake and the bracken,
Wondering if the dead still shift
The great lean leaves,
Breathing the smoke that spans
Blue dusk across deep pine,
Or streaks along too harsh...of crimson.
Wait for the drum,
A rustling rise of sound,
The grouse zagged out
And all the feathered dead,
Who for a time's loose thought
Panted clear steps
And drubbed a fragile measure
In this fall of leaves, autumn wet,
Some fragile goal spent...

◆ ◆ ◆

It is evening and the gulls are at sea.
I did not know my mother from a thin birch tree.
I did not know myself though it knew me
In the high wind, in the low wind and the shadows of the
    tree.

I would know my mother in the valley on the hill
Where the three strange crows have cawed their fill,
Where the mind lies curled like a thin ill
Hand and the high wind, low wind, valley and the hill.

High wind, low wind, and where shall I go?
It is a sad time for children as I know.
There are three strange crows that caw in a row.
I do not know my mother from a thin birch row.

All earth swellings bear a twisted peak,
As akin to the earth as to the sky.

Fingers that form the eternal child-bird
Chiseled out of the mountain in awkward adolescence,
Suspended between the sun and void—
Smiling tips that form in silence things,
Rest against the long lean temple of your heaven
And think—"Why so many half-things?
So many longings? So few fulfillments? Why fear?
Why not divine strength for those who would build?
Why not simple understanding? Why?...why? why?
The fingers that make us stand twisted
Are the fingers of a drunken god, that is why!
Drunk with the liquid of his own fouling,
Leering with green eyes at his own belly,
Rolling back the yellow fat to look upon the earth—
To look upon his pupils, his mock hobgoblins
And watch their movements, if of their own making
Yet still more of his, this squat, pink-fingered god.
Yes, I know, in my heart I called out for all life.
Yes I know, in my mind I forced and formed
Myself with my own sharp long pink finger tips—
But there are others! And still the question why?
One long piercing sigh drifts through the night,
Then back to half-reality and dusks and streams of gold
That cling, scenting my nostrils
With the heady wind of twisted peaks that spill
Tumbling through and through, the clean-swept sky
To look with awe upon the sun's still, livid, face
The little fat, squat god sitting in sad Buddhistic solitude.

The opulent sky
Holds the mirror to my thoughts,
Grey tatters wandering high
In the hollow of my head.

Yes, make a note of the way the sun sets
Make a pattern in the dry dust
It simply couldn't understand and frets
The more, this pathetic globular nonentity.

To know...to know yet not to feel!
But how extraordinarily amusing
It must make the gray sky real
And pinch its sides with kindly laughter.

The grayness of the sky lifts one smoky lid
A luminous point of light cuts along water—
And the quivering fish-belly of the sea hid
Its silver like a kiss against its side.

Oh, the labour of so few words
That should be flung like banners at the sun.
A thousand, million people, all the herds
Of creatures in the world feel simply.

To look my soul in the eyes is sad,
For I cannot exalt at nature and that is sad too.
Yes indeed, it all seems rather bad
For my sad little soul I think.

I spill my tea carelessly,
And it pearls along a point of grass,
Losing its clearness, and glowing amber dully
For a moment before sinking through earth.

This somehow all seems rather unpleasant,
A thing goes on before my eyes and I cannot follow,
Held unmercifully to the soil like a squealing infant.
What inconceivable frustration!

The sky is tinting dark blue,
Gray softening into blue along the edges.
Good God no! I'm not through.
Yet. If I lift my arms so, and wait—perhaps....?

Oh, thou all-encircling space
Enter my being, O enter this place.

I want... O God, I want to feel...
To feel... feel... feel terribly free!

See, I stretch up my arms, lift my head so high—
Till the wind hurls me crucified
Crucified?... Crucified, Why?

◆ ◆ ◆

1. Is all at least partially as you might wish?
2. Was the flat even slightly in shape to be sent off?

And O what gravity sits upon me here
Indeed I am a fellow with something of the world
    upon my shoulders.
I turn and say to you "Now I work. I earn to learn!"
Masters of thought
                    Gutkind
The Arts
                    Ozenfant
Anthropology and Culture
                    Stern
World Literature
                    Lenrow
Conflicting World Capitals
                    Kohn
I am in a library for this week and then tickets to be
    taken.
And so I might tell you more of this
Like a crow with wings that will not come down
A cock 'o the walk fluffing a pretty feather.
There is a thing I can't shake from my mind though.
That Limbo you must have automatically slipped
    me to.
I remember mentioning the fact of it to a child
In my convent days
She neatly placed me with a slight half shiver
In that gray-green unborn world
I could taste the colour—finger the dullfelt mute of a
    place.
You said, "And indeed that explains it!"

I, perhaps, see strings of nuns
Like black pearls drawn slowly t'ards the step
And well there may be a star at the top
And there are the doleful moods of my mock-goblin
    godliness.

Vermont valley where the suns spread down,
Long shadow reaching to the little town,
Where in an evening on the porch we sat,
An evening, an hour, a time,
There where we were, I'm
Counting New England dusk,
Hearing that husk.
Come up to me, Vermont valley dusk.

Vermont valley music in water,
Vermont valley, song of Adam's daughter,
And the long night breeze,
An evening, an hour, a time,
There where eyes look and meet, I'm
Counting New England dusk,
Over the blue-hilled husk,
Wrapping us here in the green evening trees,
Vermont valley dusk.

With every hour passing,
A still tiredness waits in me.
I hope you know passing
Is all that ever may be.
Not the hills with their moon shadows,
Or the moon oval and subdued,
Not the full moment of the movements that delude,
Not the hills,
Not the noon shadows,
Not hour that thrills,
Only remaining weariness.

There are various peaks.
In the evening they shine
As their points uploom and spire.
I do not want to see phantom intrusion
As desolate memoried confusion,
Rather quiet hands of day, inviolate fires.

So many women have known hills,
Children. I meeting their play
Castle, tiny over dunes, sands
Outlipping water with its voluble word,
Remarking the gull whose shrill they quite incurred
Running brisk sound to edge the narrowed land.

These immemorables, these shy or questioned shapes,
People, such slope upon the way,
Yourself who go, a wintery or an oblique hand,
Admit, clasp out, return to the private address,
The child's unnourished mouth, taut to confess
Thirst and the dark awake of natural demand,—

Bring back fear in all its places,
A tangent cat with four feet and the tail
Leaping the high black lap of night.
I shall not speak. No sun's revolution,
Sterile of head, and no fruition
Myself, I shall be as I am. Yourself, somewhere delight.

Long evenings with the widow,
Pitting resilient nipples against cold window pane,
Fought the black smooth cloth and law,
The resultant pain.

Nothing to be, nor dead, than the pass of action;
Nothing more heavy than the defunct sense of time,
Hour that gives a tradition
In the dripping of the lime,

And mouths in strange opening
Out of dead hills reach toward the widow,
And that was prattled, crying, gaping,
Lips cast to leave singing holes,
While the grasses grow.

And mounting, mounting, wearing words,
From new green, new flowing in April,
Hale eye, dreaming the birds,
Strange lipping over resilient hills...

◆ ◆ ◆

The hour like a child runs down the angle of star and rests
    at the bottom
It is a strange woman that may hold that child in its arms
But women prefer to see the hours slip from their fingers
For they are dancing an old earth constituency

I am a little beyond the river and stare from my particular
    casement
I am slender as the stalk and have my own flowering
I don't draw from women but I prefer the truth and not the
    trick of living

Therefore I walk by women as the sea ponders by the shore
I tremble and splash my spray by the cavern
Hear my own strange breath and laughter
But is my echoing and I am unalterably the sea.

◆ ◆ ◆

Think of the spring—warm in its new beauty
And of the fresh wet sky drooping against greenness
Oh yes and gleaming daffodils, clinging to the slopes
For a moment forget—and drift amongst it all—
The smooth quiet beauty of the coming spring.

Rest—here lies a wood,
Echo of blue beneath you—good!
Violets encrusted against green.
The only movement seen
A lark, rising sharply.
An old oak, reflecting darkly
Across the weed-webbed pool.
Here there is no spiritual duel.
But only sounds of silence born from the wood
The smooth, long silence of a peace that's—good.

The Dream of the Architect

The shore, the sea and the horizon.
The simplicity is broken by a half-buried tower and the
few stones from its walls about the sand.
The civilian leans against a stone.
He has various unrolled blue prints at his side.
He unrolls one plan and stares.

THE CIVILIAN
No longer will the names of angels give extension
To the cults of contrition or imitation,
The sharp hand strike or the pillar of fire
Draw from the mother shape the admitting of a virgin sire.
God, who has stamped, clapped eyes, knows nothing more
Than the hollow and excretion, the angles and the door;
The sleeping seed, the dormitories where we sleep,
And in the birdless night the creep
Amongst the pent reeds and the sound of water;
While the infants breathe deeply in a similar
Distress at strangers or cry out at the closed wings—
The wings of the alighting angels about the arid springs
Of ancient Hebrew and the bartered islands.
O there is no land that has not given—the sands
And the hidden inlets have born and thrust the sea
Back with its vagrant though into the shell of its immensity.
The angels no longer find their names upon the rim.
All that were names have become the grim
Clap, the swift action, the wretched anger.
The angels leap at man and the tireder
Gods, driving their poor white knuckles to their eyes,

Forget the wordless for a land that lies
Forever east and west and is legend memory
In the unalterable extent of that race stream tormenting to
    the sea.
Bend over the figures on this sand. We sleep here,
Each will propped with a sword above the head, the
    nameless sword of fear.

THE CHORUS OF FIVE WOMEN *(enters)*
We are the five dreams of the Unemployed Architect.
Five cities upon five hills, five arrangements of the
    intellect,
Five women of conception and delight
Structure within structure, life in life, breadth and height.

THE CIVILIAN
While you were pricking out the strange blue plan, I was
    dancing an awkward step toward the future of man.
Dancing the confusion and eruption alone,
Making sound with my bones, with my feet stamping the
    one
Drum over and over again without end.
The demand of doing well the bad would send
Me into a more than bitterness, into a very fatherhood of
    action.
Alert white forms stood by at every crumpled stair to
    sanction
The dying to carry the dead to the burial lands,
The wet shores where the waves bear out the lovers of
    earth in their hands.
There were sea gulls whenever the storms came over the
    water,
To inundate the restless places and the timeless sleeper.
The widows that gathered from the cities knelt there.

186

The sea gulls and the wives, the girls and the women
    without sons,
Their eyes on the horizon for invasion or turned to the
    farther channels
Of the sea,
Were immutable in their cold austerity
And yet, the few heard wings. The gulls beyond the rotting
    nets
Where the fisherman now gathers and lets
His sleek imaginary catch fall to the deck in that pale under
    water made the stir.
If you cannot name images or touch the shrill night crier,
Why fold hands together or shake tears from sockets warm
    with fact?
O yes, the dreadful angels have their symbol in some
    human act,
The pillar of fire takes on the soft young lad,
The witch and evil have their symbols in the ruling mad.

THE LEADER OF THE CHORUS
We have dreamt within this dream of the grandeur of detail,
In which the wayward and the frail
Exist no longer in contrast but for themselves,
As we, who are shapes and conception, have meaning in
    ourselves.

THE CHORUS OF FIVE WOMEN
We who are cool structures and the result of living,
Are filled with an endless wonder at the immense will of
    creating
That the hideous moment breathes in the air—
A small child to flick its thought off the rim of man's
    despair.

THE LEADER
Quiet: The Architect will not wake yet.
Let us sink deeper into the sleep will we have met
The unbornhour and the directless mute,
Whose song stars on with voided eyes from the primal root.

THE CHORUS OF FIVE WOMEN
Weird sleep, mother of day,
Aspect of words we sing to you.
Our voices rising lift away
The turret and the torn. The new
Time nursed on old land
Bears out the temper of its own command.

Weird sleep, mother of day,
Aspect of words we sing to you.
Remember the memory where the speechless pray,
The tired gather dancing, the few
Stand in boundless multitudes upon the hill,
While man, who wept, reclaims the instinct will?

THE CIVILIAN
I recall the building, the castles and the ornament
The swans and the unicorn, the tryst and the embattlement;
The great splashing river in the embittered dark,
The trees lurking thinly in the winter park,
The fragile inlay that flecked off into dust
With us who were too startled to protest; the strength of
    our lust
After the drum, the wind, the clock in the tower, the time
    hunger.
The love of minutes and the hours grew from our temper,
Not from the calm the mechanical thing cried out for in
    its god.

The frightful angels and the frightful anger, what good
Are these symbols that were a part of us, stood off and are
    with us again
Each in their own stark attitudes of pain?

THE LEADER
The wind blows the pale dry scent
From the streets, the dunes and the battlement.
Listen to the old complaining of their age,
Yet shouting to their knees at the bugle heritage.
Decadence is mind's end, not man, the lean fears that we
    grasp
As the drowned white bodies that the dull tides clasp.

THE CHORUS OF FIVE WOMEN
In the damp alley let the houses fall,
Into the barren arms of all
The five cities, where decay is inert,
Spinning tired webs with the hurt
Face of the spider caught
Behind the delicate scheme or the self wound plot.

THE LEADER
Now the dream of the Unemployed Architect
Turns from the introspective word to the conflict
Of idea and reality in active motion.
Unconsciously his mind draws into the cell or embryo
    construction.
He hazards the subconscious to externalize
The natural formula that lies
In the full growth and movement,
The spring's great marriage and the winter's great annul-
    ment.

The light broadens. The dancers enter. Their movements make explicit the detail and the full sweep of the Architect's scheme.

SCENE 2

There are three slender trees, the leaves so high that only the stems may be seen. The turret remains. Where the Architect lay rise the trees. The angle of light sends three shadows in bars across the sand.
The Unemployed Woman stands stiffly to one side.

THE CIVILIAN
You who came to this shore to find the child
Have wandered between the dry sands and the sea or held
The loose shells in your fists and clattered pebbles under foot.
Now men cry out against those gestures of sterility and
    long to put
Into the lovely late sun the woman's power to quiet,
To attempt once more the new young rising before the wet
Eyes of the tired expanse and its discordances.
I will gather in my arms the centuries
And you will calm them like ill children at your side.
There is no stillness and no life that you will not copulate
    with pride
In all positions of earth pregnancy.
Now in the late day, you stand alone, the fourth enigmatic
    tree

THE LEADER *(passing behind the Woman and staring at
her)*
I see you in terms of the possible,
Rather than the immediate and impossible.

THE BOY *(stretching out of the turret top, swings and drops)*

THE CIVILIAN *(mocking)*
A child is born not out of your womb, woman,
But out of the worn centuries of man.

THE BOY *(clasping an arm about a tree and also staring at the woman)*
I have rocked myself in sleep;
Hi, Ho,
Into flesh and bone I leap,
Through the gulls-craw of the deep,
Hi, Ho,
When I die the world will creep
Out of nowhere back to sleep;
Hi, Ho,

THE CHORUS OF FIVE WOMEN *(out of view and spoken in two groups)*
A beautiful mad son climbed from the damp turret.
Why were there no windows to let
The songs of small children out to open sky?

SECOND GROUP
It is because direct wisdom denies the sacrosanct lie.
We do not know how to select our fears.
Good laughter from the evil, the mock from vital tears.

THE CHORUS OF FIVE WOMEN *(enters)*
Tell us of the things you know, child,
Are you delighted with the valiant mad, and wild?

THE BOY
If I had been gentle would I have known my mother?

Clear to the sun I stretch and could not find her.
But my father was less, so that I had to turn upon myself,
Make two round images to sleep and bear me, for I would
  know this self.
The tower that you see winds down into its source
And though it seems crumpled a terrific force
Of memory breaks at the crack and throws up in the
  night.
I am not mindless but lost. I do not know the dark from
  day, the wrong from right.

THE CIVILIAN
I cannot stand the child's denial of its parent,
Or the boneless mad or the lack of intent,
Or gulls without purpose in their flight,
Or mothers who have miscarried without the contrite
Call to alleviate the anger at its source.
It is like the frantic plague that rides the horse
To its knees screaming the air into desolation.
I cannot stand the querulous child, the unboned or the
  wrecker's destruction.

THE LEADER
Beside life at its immoderate points stands the Architect.
Beside the Unemployed Woman and the neglect,
At first so apparent in the child,
The line is drawn, the dream conceived and what was
  held
To be misplaced used to further the elemental base,
The house, the word, the underprivileged race.

THE CHORUS OF FIVE WOMEN
The Woman remembering her heritage of movement,
  stirs.

The slope, the water spout, the wind are hers,
Linked and and withheld in the structure of her body.
It is a bare dance that she knows; she has thrust the tears
    inadequately,
Passed quickly over complicated cities
And stood uprooted beside these banished trees.
A dance of praise as strictly beautiful as the thought of the
Architect
Is in her mind and her arms shift to inflect
Their attitudes of direction upon the air.
The formal gesture of the brave now make self aware.

THE CIVILIAN
O remarkable woman, neither the sea drowns you,
Nor the sands draw back your bones to a few
Unaccountable grains along the shore.
I who more than deplore
Your past ask the turret to absolve you and return you to
    your child,
So that he will not be too fretful with the inadequate
    world.

THE LEADER
The dance of praise is the ritual upon ground.
It is the exact conception of the wound,
It leaves the delinquent heat behind the cloud
And is its own personal loud
Music.

THE CHORUS OF FIVE WOMEN
The panic
Tyranny and contentions go.
The lovely dance moves to a slow
Reflection, of transcending weight.

There is no reason than to do more than breathe a late
Breath, the silence cannot be broken being elastically taut.
The moment of rest caught
By the lifted face at an ecstatic angle.
Claims by its light the right to name the angel.
Let us have quiet sands where quiet objects pass,
And know a central calm divested of the mass.
Let us remain as keys unpressed though anticipating the
    touch,
Let us simply be till being we must move as something
    poised.
Released . . . vast gulls extending tantamount,
Victorious in grace and wing delight, paramount
Upon (sea and under) water (and) the songs of quiet things
    on our tongues.
The sea god cries within us, each word rising from our
    bubbling lungs.
O listen to the sound of water for it is the submerged
    memory
Disporting in pools of our tranquility
We speak with wind and water and are desolate sounds
Our movement so articulate over the hill, bounds
Into the valley of distinctions and barely startles to the will
There for drink and fill
The mute horn of silence, open the palms and stare
Into the rattled heart, the sleek lead tongue and the snake's
    abortive glare.

Yesterday I could see the parent in the oak and ash,
The slender multitudes of birch, the lingering wash
Of water beyond sleep, in the mother slope
Whose side I often pressed against through the long nights
    to avoid the lope
Of the silent hunger. Even willing that thing

To be wolf-mother I would suddenly sing
Out with an odd music. Together sitting back on stiff
    haunches
We wailed with the same pain, the same terrible aches
That lie in that eternal loneliness borne of blood and bone.
The insect and the bird, the tree, the beast, the stone, called
    me their son, their child, I thought. Or was it I that
    named them parent?

THE CHORUS OF FIVE WOMEN
O lament
Wind. 'For this is a wise but unclaimed child.

THE BOY
Stand at the cliff top wild
With the wish to be wanted by the nesting gull:
One cannot be wise without some edge and I am full
Of a wisdom from rejection.
Having stood alone on hills and sprung down valleys with
    distraction
One day I found that I had come upon my own thin shape,
Startled I leapt away attempting to escape.

THE CHORUS OF FIVE WOMEN
We can see you as you speak of it.
A small astounding figure struggling with wind and water,
    hit
By shrilling birds, your hands before your face
Running the extraordinary race
Against your small boy's form and the being something else
    than sea
And wind and fawn, or the shoot from the mother tree.
Then at last the pause, the searching of reflections,
And in the mind again the question, queries and deductions,

For it seemed the parent was unfound and the uneven
   country barely covered.
Your child's eyes darkly closed, that night you left round
   pools where you had slept and cried.

THE BOY

Now knowing my own shape I wondered at my use.
I was innocent and unborn once again, free to muse
With a difference upon rock.
Free with a freedom that ran to meet me with the shock
Of new angers and new loves immediate and my own.
I knew that I was a part within a purpose,
And here rose the first movements of those
Awakening man-dissemblers, emotion and the brain.
O I did not know a right from wrong and therefore seemed
   insane.
What was it that threw me from the height
Down the opened vein of land into the night
Of ghosts, chanting women and distorted men
Into the centre smoke and flame then
Dragged off from the mind to flesh, from hand to head,
Every moment claimed and reborn from a male and female
   dead
And the past history that took my namelessness,
Shooting me as a life, an answer and an act, less
For myself than their own wide meaning.
There were high words chanting.
What was it said? That I was born of men, not man!
I was sad yet laughed and touched the wall for windows. An
Air of tenseness loomed. The faces watched the act.
I sang, I danced, the weight of past had driven out the fact.
The mad child's vision made me like a reed
And playing my own music I was flung from the tired
   turret, time's ejected seed.

SCENE 3

Along the shore. Only the flat sky are to be seen. The
    Unemployed
Woman makes the last movement of the dance.
The Architect lies before her working on his plans. They
    are both unconscious of the terrible wind that blows.
The plans fly from the Architect's hands.
The Boy catches them as he enters.
He leaps with delight.

THE CHORUS OF FIVE WOMEN *(Off. They talk roundly
over the wind)*
The child does not know what cities it gathers,
What lives it holds and the innumerable lovers.
It does not know the father and the mother or the hard
    blowing wind.
Its self delight will not attend
To the grave face of the parent and the inscrutable hour,
Or grasp the intent of those that claim to power.
It is only when the two who wait upon the shore
Realize they have deflected more
Energy than they know from the void into the world,
That we shall hear this lad proclaimed the rightful child.

THE BOY
Wind, Wind! I shall be a juggler of red balls,
I shall sit on a rock looking out with my eyes,
And I shall know all the shapes and edges.

Wind, Wind! I shall be a juggler of little animals
I shall sit in a tree and pluck thoughts,
Or I shall be glad and simply clap my hands.

THE CHORUS OF FIVE WOMEN
Can you see with your eyes the two upon the beach?
Beg them to bring you out of the wind and within reach
Of memory, into the very stream of their projected minds.
Beg them to take you as you are out of the variant winds;
Must it be said that the Unemployed breed the miscella-
    neous,
Thrust from their sides the unwanted infant with a
    reckless
Hand having forgotten the wonderful journey
Towards those uncharted islands of the sea?

THE BOY
Knowing my own shape I wondered at my use
I was innocent and unborn once again, free to muse
With a difference upon rock.
Free with a freedom that ran to meet me with the shock
Of new angers and new loves immediate and my own.
I knew that I was a part within a purpose
And realized the first awakening of those
Dissemblers, emotion and the brain.
Though I could not tell a right from a wrong and therefore
    seemed insane
What was it that flung me from the height
Down the open vein of land into the night
Of ghosts, enchanted women and cavorting men,
Into the centre smoke and flame then
Dragged me on from flesh to mind, from hand to head
The every moment claimed and reborn from a male and
    female dead
And the past histories that took my namelessness,
Calling me life, the new, the answer and the act, less
For myself than their own wide meaning.
There were high words and so much loud chanting

Would I admit this dead? Would the dead admit me? I who
    was born
That day of men not man?
Sad yet I laughed and felt their walls for windows. An
Air of tenseness loomed. The faces watched the act.
I sang, I danced, the weight of past had driven out the fact
The mad child's vision made me like a reed
And playing my own music I was flung up from the turret,
    time's ejected (sea) or (seed)

◆ ◆ ◆

Woman whose body
As a deep tuned earth
Needs at my eager side
Pulsing a swift move
O against my loin and against my breast
What is the womb you hold me to
I am in the seed of you
Dumb-embryo still with mute eyes
Unthinking sucked back to sea
Into the dark groined-past
Or with a feeble mouth sipping
Still memory from your
High swung breasts
Your full blocked womanness
And always the seed of you
Panting the seed of me.
Onto my lips my child-life
And all the cavern of a space? Ran
Soundless without your step.

◆ ◆ ◆

(In the voice of a young black boy, sung to a lute)

Black people, you listen to me,
Black people, I've got something to say.
Do you feel that high wind from tomorrow?
A woman all undressed and admitting herself.
That's what tomorrow blows.

I'm a singing child with my hands plucking.
I don't even know my beginning and why.
I love anyhow, anywhere,
I see sea-birds fall and catch,
And the moon means something to me.

Black people, look all about the placid stars.
Look after your growing and your nights.
Know that a girl's side hard against you starts up into life.
How much you belong to this earth is how sweet your
    song is.
Black people, nobody belongs to the earth as you do.

I'm a child. That's how long my life is.
That's how dark and how light it is too.
I don't see anyone much older.
Lions at the zoo pain always at the bars.
Black people, do you listen to what I say?

When moonlight skies are new
To brushing kids at night
That sweep an ivory slip of star
Like trembling skies that lift
A cry sifts high through clouds
Passing leaves like new days by.

Circling, a mighty sigh lifts
Once again on high
To light and dawning sky.
Stretch out upon a day,
Upon a day of days and by.

Oh, let the world roll on.
There's nothing more to say,
But here the song is sung,
Then tossed upon a thought
To rest where all is gone
And blue lights flicker by.

◆ ◆ ◆

Build the churches high and straight
Architects are always late
Every moment counts with man
Brief or edgeless be his plan.
Watch the water lick the dike
What we wish and what we like
Find it in a ruthless sea
A church for you and a church for me
God be praised the church has gone
Man has whistled over lone
In the empty churchyard so
Where has God gone we don't know.
Every little son of day
Watch the little girls at play
Know you are a little man
Let's all dance now if we can.
Architects build that home
Out of churchyards out of loam
Up where stars are
Out where cars are
Give us babies
And less maybes
For a race
Some place
For a day
Some play

In the evening over the well curved hills
He stared,

In his mornings he would trace leaves
Their shape,

In his mornings and listlessly tracing
Himself, seeing his face where shadows stopped
And hearing his name in many bird throats
He had the desire to remove the cause for such repetition

Pushing grass aside he found a pool, the pool
The weeds closed the reflection from him
He frowned. Better to have seen the face
That to feel it lurking there below, and himself hid from
Him.

Stirring the fetid surface his eye wandered
His purpose almost dropping to the side.
A woman in the reeds placed her hand against him
He sank mournful with his name upon the air.

◆ ◆ ◆

Leaves winter leaves where do you blow
Where the winds take you there I go
Softly dance softly summer has gone
Other loves lure me old loves are done.

Snow flakes are slipping
Cold winds nipping
Dry leaves dancing
Winter romancing.

Snow queens bend from the high pine tree
Where the bows bend there you'll find me.
Slender each shade as it sways to the sound
The mutter of winter the snow queen's crown

Snow flakes are slipping,
Cold winds nipping,
Dry leaves dancing
Winter romancing.

Leaves winter leaves where do you blow?
Where the winds take you there go
Of the cry the old suns die
Sleek are my sloped where the new loves lie.

Song

Life, life, life!
Time flies on pointed heels,
Sharp are they to him who feels,
Loud the church bell harshly peals
At night.

Life, life, life!
There are no church bells here,
Where the pipes of Pan ring clear.
No passing time draws passing near,
No night.

Life, life, life!
You pipes of life play on,
Lift up that rim of rising dawn,
We'll dance and sing till night has gone
Into the night.

◆　◆　◆

You like stars bless!
Incomprehensible rays
Conforming to a certain,
Pulled with unmanacled
Hands toward my lips,
A certain strain.
Sometimes they blur,
People fade to mist
Far and meaningless.
The pale face gone.
The hair cloud spent,
At the shrill sigh
Of a broken knot
The hair remembered
The face well drawn
To white opaque docility
Of outfused line
Where once puck tranquility
Disturbed the mind
In severity of substance,
I remember that you
Like stars are blessed!

Vision in Arcaid

1
The long crisp taffeta of trees
Stemming themselves against the breeze!

2
"Will you tell me where the dimpled lawn
The nimble tread of a dappled fawn...?
An obscure bird with a lilt and trill
Has echoed the call between hill and hill?"
The happy lad with a languid air,
Ran his hands through his out-spun hair.
Stopped to finger a sudden thought
In the gold brocade where the thread had caught

3
"Ancient, ancient are the ruined walls.
Old the spire, arched and vacant halls,
Where, with hands swung loose between the knees
Yet still in a moment as an oaken freeze,
A figure inanimate and grey
Turns up his face to meet the gathering day
Through the high translucent window-pane
With its three quiet saints in coloured-stain
Of an old and timeless beauty,
Of an old and timeless beauty."

4

And again the leaves rustle through his head,
And off is the lad where his thoughts have sped,
And naked the lad he looks upon,
Spawn of the night and the querulous dawn,
Whose windowed saints in purple and gold
And the crimson cowls and the crooks they hold,
The benign glance and the lifted host,
(O sweet bacchanal of Holy Ghost!)
Look but gently upon the lad,
While the wind whispers thoughts that are ancient and sad
And filled with a timeless beauty,
Of an old and timeless beauty.

5

Green is the grass and subtle the slope
Still as the breath in a moment's hope.
The monotonous dip and dipping bird
Tilts a note to the lowing herd.
Then up lad up O on your way
For spent is the time, ill spent the day!

Lines to Various Modern Authors

Lean and peaked as a child,
You grew to man with a preoccupied look.
All that your youth had pined and piled
Resulted in a book.

Who could disclaim your place within the day,
Whether your sun was full or bleak?
Whether you jerked with caustic wit or some more
    crass display.
Who could disclaim your right within the clique?

Ulysses

Time fumbled around the corner—
Moons were lit,
Sky-dimmed trees faded beneath the sea.
I lifted my eyes to the heavens
And sang of things—
Dim mists, stars, and sun-tossed worlds
Lost in morning dews—
And craggy long-lived rocks above the margins.
Spinning life ran down space—
Clawing through smeared fogs,
And stretched itself flat across the earth,—
Bowing below the ragged edge
Of night's first hollow glow.
Thin storm-tossed dreams wisped across
The flat-faced moons—
Heads bent and withered arms outstretched,
Grasping for the sun's first warm embrace—
That died before it grew.
Soft woman clung about my heart—
A fear that grew sweet in its pain.
Yet far pleasanter than others
That cried in their cradles, MAN!
Gray eyes poured into mine—
Hope yet no hope,
I beat weakly against the fates—
Then gladly welcomed them—
In a hidden shaft within my soul.

Jingle

A twisting of yellow on the sea-green floor,
Dripping of a cool sun through the open door.
Smooth curve of birds wings clipping through the sky
That, taut blue and glinting, quivers as they fly.

Green and gold, green and gold singing through the air.
Two larks leaping from their purpled lair—
Bubbling, quick-burbling, clear tumbled notes,
Lisping and wisping from their throbbing throats.

White, rippled silver smoothed across blue.
Sea-dipped green tanglings with gold splashing through.

Fata Morgana

To wander aimlessly
And the breeze too
To wander aimlessly
And to brush against...
Ah, to brush the edge
Of my skin
As I wander aimlessly.

The sun riddling through
To dark grass.
Letting its feet
Slip quietly through
And patter mellowly
Against leaf-green
To grass-green.
Against grass-green
To leaf-green pattering.

Softly a crystal shadow
Smooths before me.
To wander aimlessly,
To come upon iridescence
And to see a crystal...
To see a crystal shadow.
This is a dream... Yes!
A cloud softly breathing,
Languorously sleeping.
The pink of half formed...
(Slipping through silver,)
Of half-formed life—
This is ecstasy!

To wander aimlessly
And the breeze too
To wander aimlessly
And brush against...
Ah, to brush the edge
Of my skin
As I wander aimlessly.

◆　◆　◆

And so with a sunk and oozing eye
I slip along the dank stone-way
Letting my sadness drip to a sadder rondelay
To the drip drip drip of its lay
Under the cloying green sea way
                    to drip to a darker rondelay

Doomed to the cloistered corridors
Slipped along in the baroque light
Chilled and shadowed the shadowing night
Churned to the wind-churned sea in flight
Beyond the day and out of the night
And under the cloying green sea way
                    drip to the darker rondelay

Here where the cracks are slimy smooth
I throw back my head and my pale washed eyes
Piercing the rifts to the vacant skies
Circling the rock where the old hulk lies
And the drift of my form where the white spray flies
Then down once more to the green sea way
                    drip to the roll of the rondelay

Deo Gratias Deo Gratias ad infinitum
For my soft flesh sides are a tomb of gold
And the cold grey stretch of my arms bare gold
While my free swung breasts are a diamond mold
And the gold of my hair I can hardly hold
Weighed so deep in the green sea way
                    jeweled tears drip to the rondelay

And so with a hollow half-spent sigh
I sway to the void and the seaweeds sway
Seeped through the deep halls caverned way
Gone with the moon mists dip to the lay
Under the cloying green sea way
                    to drip to a darker rondelay

Shepherd Boy's Lament

My soul is a faun surmising,
My mind a steel-lined shell,
My flesh the weight of pyramids
And I am a little sad.

My love has the soul of a faun,
Her arms are two white lilies
Burning in the moonlight—
Tracing the sharp curve
Of the North Star softly,
And I am a little sad.

I stretch my young boy limbs
Down by the side of my sheep—
Little white sheep-hillocks
Bursting from the earth
Like small white breasts.

The air is weighted with dung-smell,
The grass rustles,
My sheep press heavily
Against the ground
And I am a little sad.

In a little while, dawn is here,
But my faun soul is still sleeping,
And the night is so jealous
Of her secrets.
If I pray, my mind wanders—
It is so empty, this song.

My love has the soul of a faun,
And her form glows like a star,
And the stars drift through her form.
Yes, my love is a mist of stars,
And I am a little sad.

Wantastiquet

A river twist and water pebble pitted.
Where in the West River did rubble splinter
From its instoned source?
A brief move in clear immensity
Chuckled and chuffed the stuff
Made marble mud and rock clatter down
Down the great veined arm
And meeting of the mother.
Pebbles wet and slattern slagged
Bouldering in the Great Eyed on Connecticut.

The throbbing sob of dance night things,
The sometimes relaxed, sometimes vital sounds
Of people spilling out thought
In the glow of a still coal fire...
All day an opaque tear has bubbled softly
And now in the night it seeps and flows in my body,
Aching consciously and dully,
Surging ceaselessly, like the slow grey thud of sea waves.
It has a tune all its own, this monotonous pain,
And the words beat, beat, beat in my brain,
Like waves, like great god-hammers
Desire, ambition, frustration, the pain!

◆ ◆ ◆

Pearl lustered
Dropped and held
Slipped through
And Pressed
Quietly

The pale moon's breasts
Are rivers of reflection
To this thought
Where the edge of vision
Returns toward the edge

Soon another moon has rolled
And so they go
Trees finger the new dawn
But a new day has wings
And wind in its wings
And with the night a dream
A song to sing
A shy quick hand to shadows
A cry
And then again
Abandonment
Silence
A breath
A smile
Perhaps a song well sung
Well dreamed
Will hesitant to will
That leaps

A dream traced by the tip
Of mind
And dropped

Double-Trouble

Chorus.
Wherever I look
There's another of me,
Double or triple ten to three.

You double-trouble hold me tight
Don't leave me for this one night.
One and one makes two,
What Noah said is true
Just ask them at the zoo.

Chorus.
Wherever I look
There's another of me,
Double, triple ten to three.

That's better, honey, turn this way,
My heart beats double time.
Two nickels make a dime,
A dime makes a song and dance
A sigh and some romance.

Chorus.
Wherever I look
There's another of me,
Double, triple ten to three.

The Rose

You are clear,
O rose cut in rock.
Hard as the descent of hail.

I could scrape the color
From the petals
Like spilt dye from a rock.

If I could break you
I could break a tree.

If I could stir
I could break a tree
I could break you.

A Tear

Memories whispering into relief
Awakening the shadows of childhood belief,
Bursting on, growing vividly clear,
Bright atom of crisp turning fear!
Look! Shadows painted,
Carved from souls that fainted
On the eternal path down.
Withered leaves of the glowing brown
Burn on a little longer
Till a tear once again envisions her
Who is built in the mind
Like a pale star that will never find
The peace that world intimatings planned
For chiseled fools of the promised land.
Rocks towering above create
The true feeling of the depth of fate.
And so she cried out, tired leaf against green,
Green so passionately sad as if it had been
Dipped through all the caverns of a haunted sea
Till, brushing itself heavily,
It lay smeared, a background for one solitary tear.
This picture even here
It painted from the palette of a jungle night,
Of a being that half caught the light,
Half caught a star, half caught the hollow echo in the roof
Of heaven, that wisps between sun and moon, the truth!

❖ ❖ ❖

O' light that kneels across the sea—
True image of the Mighty God—
Spirit that climbs into our ghosts
And ladens them with gold—
Answer my desire—
Fame!—A love of all and both—
That I may feel all life,
And see a thousand seas of truth! and so I shall clothe
    myself
In ambition
Rather than face the world naked.
And live a life of struggle—joy and pain
Forever and forever
'Till all things die.

◆ ◆ ◆

Their daughter is there alone as she must be
Remember the dark sadness of the cypress tree.
While there is time and our hands are sick of plucking
Tilt out your shoulders in timeless running
Feel the still ledge and banking to the water
As something never yours but only of this daughter.
There is slope to the hill and in the distance
Hear the passing of water offer strange stones
Know now your shadow and your limit in this expanse.

Do not compromise the illegitimate
Whether it is time for a woman or a word.
Ask for attentions and ingratiate
The unbranched bird.

♦ ♦ ♦

What I cannot forget in memory are the unbreakable
    pictures
Just as I cannot forget a man flushing like a girl
Or an awkward adolescent girl moving along the street
In an autumn wind

♦ ♦ ♦

Jewish woman leaning over a basket of thin sheaves

One two three spun from another day's thin light
Grow little one grow little one from the still grave
(She smoothes back the ears as if it were gold hair)
I've seen children grow round and smooth of less
All seeds for the reaping stars seeds for the reaping
Ruth gathered gleanings and my gleanings turn to bread
(She sways humming in a thin off nasal voice.)

◆ ◆ ◆

All is shrill and bright with men to fallow in
And the far dignity about has never
Would never die for love of us.
And the great dignity of sea and land would never
And the great dignity of sea and land has not wept

Indeed and the dignity of land has small love left
    for the weeping.

As worlds connived and merchant London burned
An old strength reached out for its maturity.
With something of race I stood and so discerned
The kilted island clan and highland dignity.

◆ ◆ ◆

A boy whose hair is wheat yellow
Who has stretched under the sun in good places
Knowing more than one set of hills
Maddening the slattern

◆ ◆ ◆

Shadow sublimated ride thyself
Monk of moonless riddled nights
Where freak of sleep is the one
Incandescent dark of dark night
Well then repeat what gods are saying
To me like rat-tat on skull and stone
Mark ever this remarkable contumely
That is my own

◆ ◆ ◆

Like a bell the sounds of the trees are moving
Lair on lair the one tone for the many
In the winter wind we sit and shiver
So few leaves are whirling that we count them
We perceive between the great gong wind their dryness
And the smooth pond's quiet mutation.

The walls are cast—unbent
And men with great sweating muscles
Angle on from a million span below
Or swing and hump
Hot-hitting thumb-tacked girders
With the rattatat thin steeled finger
Man with two hands building
Building a reach that sticks erotic
Up toward the full-gap-sky

❖ ❖ ❖

One day as I gazed far above the salient mountaintops
And there across the smooth vibrant sea that lay before me
I felt the true rightness of myself and all my dreams.
Up there my being caught and drifted with the passing
    clouds
Reflected the sun-bronzed peaks, the cool blueness—
I possessed everything within me—King of Kings, Master
    of all worlds.

◆ ◆ ◆

I walked by the waters
But only footsteps were heard
For the night was muffled
There was a dipping of light
Swept there by silent watcher
And if my voice cried out
It grew bleakly beyond
Darkness
The moon traveled on
And looked through green shadows
Where water lilies drooped
And slept against quiet waters

I Am My Deep Sunk Womb

I am sucked in the earth to my belly
O father—Pregnant with black seed!
Bearing always a ripeness and a fruition
By the side of the he-ox
I bow submissive in my thought
Knowing that all this weight and retch of my thighs
Will sometime swell the lift of the harvest land.

Willow do not always weep delicately
By the hill slope I and three willows
Neither gazed at the reflection of our pale complexions
Nor tangled the sheaves of silver green forefingers
That made up the space between
The crisp dulled cloth and hair
Willows sometimes fling with splendid disarray
The melancholy chastity to the winds and the
Sky
As if

◆ ◆ ◆

Through doors and windows
Shadows drift in early spring
Even the spilt wine of the weight
Is like the shadow of the hurried yesterday
Clear cut green leafed trees
Echo their quietness in their dusk
Leaping again to a quickened life
That comes with the wind
To muffle out as quickly as it came

◆ ◆ ◆

Neither that that you may see
Released in that nor me
Quiet might it be alone with stars
As that which scatters sometimes mars
A cloud amorphous dies a death
A little chatter drives that death
Blind to the very light that once began
And feebly drifts where feeble drifts drift on
A burden smell well to high heaven's son
A putrid god at best that best denies
And so man dies
                    Methuselah

◆ ◆ ◆

The trees hang lustrous arms smooth-barked
In dappled form the trunks high-stalked
And here, the tread of minute feet
Amber wings thin-humming fleet.
O sun, soft sun, pattern the peacock sloping lawn
Draw three fine fingers surpliced faun
And twist about your angled head
"Domini, Domini!" sweetly said
A half-pucked look a foam flecked sigh
The crunch of stems and hooves that fly.
Slant bent skull ride down the leaves
Ripe as dee-dung in the autumned sheaves.

Foreword to Poems *(1947)*

I SHOULD LIKE to think that the day will come when the mere fact that a poet is published in the Yale Series of Younger Poets will be recommendation enough. I am somewhat doubtful about the present practice of having a new poet introduced to the public by an older one because my personal reaction as a reader to an announcement of a volume of poems with a foreword by somebody else is a suspicion that the publishers are afraid that the poems are not very good and want reassurance.

Nor do I care much for that so frequently used adjective "promising." If by "promising" one means, "These poems are no good in themselves but lead me to believe that you will write good ones in time," then the poems should not be published, and their author should be expected to wait till he has justified the critics' belief by producing some good poems. One should never publish work of which one thinks poorly just to encourage the author; genuine talent is tougher than that. If, on the other hand, by "promising" one means, "These poems are good and lead me to believe that you will continue to develop and write more good poems, probably quite different from these," that is something which can be said of every real poet at any stage in his career; if his work ceases to be promising in this sense, he has ceased to be a poet.

In the present instance, I should like to emphasize this point because Miss Joan Murray died at the age of twenty-four. We are not publishing her poems out of charity, because she will never be able to write any more, but because they are good, and I hope that the reader will approach her work just as objectively as if she were still alive, and not be distracted by sentimental speculation about what she might have written in the future which was denied her.

Nearly every good poet has certain emotions and imagery which recur and predominate in the work; that is what makes parody possible, and bad poetry, it should be remarked, cannot be parodied because there is no original version and manner to exaggerate. So, in Miss Murray's poetry, the dominant emotion is, I think, a feeling of isolation, and her characteristic images tactile shapes which reassure her that "Here" and "There" are both real and related to each other. In her own words: "We were lovers of things beyond our bodies."

But a critical discussion of poetry presupposes that the reader is already well familiar with the text, and is therefore out of place, I think, in the case of a new poet who has still to be read. I shall merely suggest to anyone who picks up this volume in a bookstore to open it and read, say, "You Talk of Art," "An Epithalamium," "Even the Gulls of the Cool Atlantic," and "Orpheus." I am confident that, if he is a true judge and lover of poetry, he will neither leave the store without taking the volume with him, nor ever regret his purchase.

—*W. H. Auden*

Notes

POEMS (1947)

This volume was selected by W. H. Auden in his first year of tenure as the judge of the Yale Series of Younger Poets Competition, and edited by Grant Code. I have noted differences in the titles of the poems between this edition, which restores them to the original title or the first line of untitled poems, and Code's titles in the Yale edition (indicated as GC below). Other notes include dates that appear on the original manuscripts, as well as select variants for poems in which significant changes appear between drafts of the poems. Lastly, certain spelling changes where the illegibility of the original word required guesswork are also noted.

"IF, HERE IN THE CITY, LIGHTS GLARE FROM VARIOUS SOURCE,": GC titled "If Here in the City."

THIS MAKES FOR WAR!: Titled "As It Should Be" in *Poems* (1947).

"YOU THINK YOU COMPLAIN OF THE UGLINESS OF PEO-PLE.": GC titled "One Morganatic Leer."

"THERE'S A SMALL TALE I'D LIKE TO TELL YOU HERE. A BIT SAD I BELIEVE.": GC titled "A Small Tale with Interruptions." Changed from "smell" to "small." "He used to a small little pub": This phrase may be a shorthand typo that left out "go to," as in "He used to go to a small little pub."

"THREE MEN SAT AT A MILLSTONE TABLE": GC titled "Study for an East Side Ballad." Changed "cannied" to "candied"; "Hone" changed to "Hon'."

"THE OBLIQUE CHAPELS OF THE GOTHIC,": GC titled "Dreams of a Modern Architect: I. Gothic." Titled (in pencil): "Dreams of a Modern Architect: Gothic I." Changed "spummy" to "spumey."

"THE STARVED HOUSES WITHOUT BRINKS OR PEOPLE": GC titled "Dreams of a Modern Architect: II. Starved Houses." Titled in another draft "Dreams of an Unemployed Architect." *Poems* (1947) includes a stanza from an earlier draft that combines two other drafts:

> The dog lopes through and squats beside the fire.
> And there is a place for good wine and for pacing,
> And working his plans and prints and city tower.
> The unemployed architect employed in tomorrow's tracing.

"THE MAN WHO SMILES AND TOTTERS WITH THE RIVETER": GC titled "The Riveter's Helper."

"SLEEP LITTLE ARCHITECT IT IS YOUR MOTHER'S WISH": GC titled "Lullaby."

"YOU TALK OF ART OF WORK OF BOOKS": GC titled "You Talk of Art."

"WHAT CAN I DO METHUSELAH YOUR TIME IS MINE": GC titled "What Can I Do, Methuselah?" Changed "nale" to "nail."

ON DIT!: GC titled "They Say."

EGO ALTER EGO: Changed "machedy" to "machete."

TO W. H. AUDEN: GC titled "You, Held in the Thin Cusp of Night"; he also combined material from two drafts. Alternative draft of poem has same first stanza but continues as follows:

> Turrets of words and words and the structure of your head.
> Grammatical sense a wide web,

Coolness and fragility barely giving life to the somehow dead,
Somehow dead, knowing its second nature to be more ebb
Than flow, more go than come and yet to come must go—
All that is river, be it high or low.

Lift your hair up to stand between the fingers,
Touching knowledge of leaves, anatomy, dark hours.
Not so much energy lies there as potential energy,
Not so much of tree and flower as their potential powers.
Ideas of people, pennies to tired singers
Whose fluctuant song haunts out the young man's memory.

These acts, fears and several vises,
I am I's that stand alone or chance a stranger's careless dice,
Raise for a race such paralytic voices
As God has become used to and men hear in white mice.
Typist fingers strike your hair, use unscabbered pen,
For idiots age or virulent time must succumb to a deep
    mute men.

Look at the shallow surface and be granite and limbed body
Swing more than adder tongue or mother feeling.
With hands that are unringed, unsoft and slender.
In heart be the thing that flexes before leaping,
Lean at your city window as rounded sun to a sea
And though mind is act between shadow to shadow night
    shall admit its subtle shadower.

POEM: FOR DAI: GC titled "As the Summer Sun Comes Down
into the Autumn Trees." Dedicated to Dai Newton of the
Newton family in Rockledge, with whom Murray lived for a
time and became very close.

POEM: GC titled "Three Mountains High."

"THINGS THAT ARE SINUOUS ARE THE RIVERS OF THE
LAND": GC titled "Things That Are Sinuous" in *Poems* (1947).

SPRING: "Toetarion" might be a typo of "totalitarian," "Tatarian," or, as GC has it, "total." Since none of these options seems convincing, the original has been left as a neologism or crypt word. Changed "vanting" to "vaunting." GC published what seems to be drafts of two parts of the same poem as two separate poems, "Spring" and "Improvisation for Spring." The poem in this edition treats the two parts as a single poem. Another variant of the second part of the poem runs:

O, but there is a laughing spring
With its head back and its mouth wide;
Square breasts and the masculine swing
To its every leap and stride.

There is a mountain of energy,
And the drop and flare of spray:
That is tomorrow, not torrid lethargy,
Not whimpering April, but tumultuous May.

Willows snap the too smoothed slope,
The birch knifes through the night
And lilies shout within their fragile scope.
The every phase of sweet is put to flight.

Sap flies high to the head of it all,
In a leaping drunk from winters,
Tattered leaves, the embittered fall—
Ice to the bone, to the life, in jagged splinters.

Spring, the cudgel flaying soft the land,
Swaggering all-world-wide across the sky;
Lifting waves from sea to the hard bruised sand,
Laughing earth abrupt from the wake of things that die.

VERMONT AND THE HILLS AND THE VALLEYS: Dated "August 20, 1938."

TALK OF PEOPLE IN WARNING: Changed from "Hyste" to "Hythe."

AN EPITHALAMIUM: MARRIAGE POEM FOR AN AGE: GC titled "An Epithalamium." "Epilogue," handwritten, beneath the title. "Chant" is handwritten several times between stanzas, as if directions to the reader/performer. "Neuter" is nearly illegible; it may also be "nurture" or "nature."

"THERE IS A ROCKY JUT, FLUNG LIKE A DISC": The only poem from the 1947 edition where the original manuscript is missing, and thus appears here unchanged.

"TIME WAS LIKE THE SNAIL IN HIS CUPOLAED HOUSE": Changed "taled" to "told."

"THERE IS SIMPLE PROMISE TO BE PUT FORWARD.": GC titled "A Child's Meditation and Prayer After Not Dying."

"THERE HAS BEEN MORE THAN BEGINNING AND END TO FACE.": Changed "Leisure satanic sloue and roud despond" to "Leisure satanic slow and rude despond."

"MEN AND WOMEN ONLY HAVE MEANING AS MAN AND WOMAN": Changed "ord" to "word." Murray might have intended "order."

"IN THE NIGHT WE PEOPLED EVIL FORESTS,": GC titled "Poem Into Sleep."

"INSTINCT AND SLEEP YOU ARE TWO PASSAGES THAT CONVERGE": GC titled "Instinct and Sleep."

"RIVER OF LIGHT": Changed "c, earn" to "clear" in the phrase "new clear bell of green." Changed "Calase" to "Calais."

"EVEN THE GULLS OF THE COOL ATLANTIC RETIP THE SILVER FOAM,": GC titled "Even the Gulls of the Cool Atlantic." First published in *Chimera: A Literary Quarterly* III, no. 2 (Winter 1945), as "Poem."

OF WINGS: GC titled "Where There Are Wings Contrite." Dated summer 1937.

"OF PLAINS OF SAND THAT SPEND THEMSELVES": Changed "uendo" to "innuendo."

POEM: GC titled "It Is Not I Who Am Sleeping in the Rock." On June 11, 1944, according to Murray's wishes, this poem was read while her ashes were spread by her mother and Dai and Edna Newton under the pine trees around St. John's in the Wilderness Episcopal Church, located along the Adirondack Trail near Saranac Lake. Murray instructed Dai during her final illness, "Read and then scatter the ashes to the lovely hills."

THE COMING OF STRANGE PEOPLE: Variant ending:

My city what an ugliness I have given you.
Earth there is no gentle shaping of the clay—
Time, no building in the hour.
Things come and the sea is sea without us.
All is brash and shrill with bone to fallow on
And bitter of mouth are we flavour the green
This green of spring.

POEM: GC titled "The Speed of Planes Was Still upon the Noon."

ON LOOKING AT LEFT FIELDS: Murray writes in a letter to her mother that these stanzas consisted of epigrams written as an exercise prompted by Auden that she then combined into this poem. The original prompt from Auden may have been given to her during his fall 1940 seminar at the New School, "The Language and Technique of Poetry."

"LONDON SITS WITH HER HANDS CUPPED": GC titled "London."

"ILFRACOMB IS A SEA TOWN WHERE ROCKS ELBOW": GC titled "Empire Now Dead and Mayflower." A significant alternative draft has this extended variant ending:

Mayflower with so many angling their eyes
A way from the early home toward the Cape
Wild in their look their mouths wet with sea and bitter
     sights

From various direction of the wind that filled sail
No where the today man cries may he escape
Wherever his hands would feel and know the water thin and
    frail

A sailor balanced on the spar
And even the full will wind you far
Even the slow heave of the whale
Lifting the gunwale with its tail
O my love what sea has found you
In the salt nights sea deep floor.
A sailor balanced on the spar
Blue eyed squat an English tar
O my love forever lost
The boat and spar forever tossed,
An English tar.

An English man and down to the leaving boat
We were Empire and now we are dead or Mayflower
Now our faces are old ballads shaping themselves afloat
And so many bubbles with fish wanes and with sleep
Ilfracomb is a child village that towers
With lean shapes with waves washing through deplete

I am these shores I am my past the village and the hill
Wherever sea comes with its distance opened
Out to the end and edge precipitate the will
The Cape the fishing boat the dunes only the water comes
Only that to be with to be run into and drowned
To be bared in breast of what has been running to sea

Only to be what one was one is and one becomes.

Again I saw in the clear icy spring
Lives I had lived and many people before me
Nothing of man or god has relieved the sting
Of departure from other coast and cliffs
Rigging strung like a bow arrowed irresolutely
We with the bone dry throats flung in the strange man's skiffs

"THERE IS A BURSTING OF THE PULSE OF TIME": Dated Wednesday, June 17, 1936.

"AND AS I CAME OUT FROM THE TEMPLES AND STARED": Changed "gzyng" to "gazing." Changed "S u vere" to "Severe."

JEW AMONGST RUINS: Dated January 1938.

"THE CAVES ARE SAD WHERE THE ARCHEOLOGISTS STOOD": Changed "animic" to "anemic."

"'PENELOPE!'": Changed "lisiverous" to "luciferous."

ORPHEUS: THREE ECLOGUES: First published in *Decision: A Review of Free Culture* I, no. 4 (April 1941), edited by Klaus Mann and prefaced with this note by Auden: "While collecting, at the Editor's request, material from which to select a small anthology of unpublished Poems, Miss Murray's poem came into my hands. I think it such a remarkable piece of work that I have asked *Decision* to print it as a feature (special) and to defer the anthology to some future issue."

LETTERS AND PROSE

Murray was a prodigious letter writer. A collection of her letters of some seven-hundred-plus typed pages was prepared by GC and can be found in her archive. GC and Murray's mother had intended to publish them in multiple volumes alongside *Poems* (1947). All of the letters included in this edition were taken from GC's edited manuscript of Murray's work, *A Faun Surmising*.

LETTERS TO HELEN ANDERSON: July 7, 1937: Another possibility for "demon" is "faun." "Gimlet" in the phrase "gimlet eye" is a guess of an indecipherable, typed-over word; an alternate possibility is "gourmet." At the end of the letter, GC adds a note that quotes Helen Anderson on Murray: "She insisted she was evil and monstrous and I found her what she was— lovely and wonderful."

LETTERS TO W. H. AUDEN: Undated: GC estimates August 1940. It's not clear which—if any—of the existing drafts of this letter Murray sent to Auden. In other versions of this letter, Murray omits the thank-you note of the last paragraph. June 9, 1941: An early, incomplete draft of this letter dated May 1941 has several passages that Murray omitted from the draft of June. They strongly indicate her sense of affinity with Auden, as can be seen in these two poignant paragraphs:

> You had mentioned once an affinity. I myself had never any doubt about that. The difference may lie in the fact that you are articulate while I remain unevolved or laboring under so many inessential details.
>
> I had been thinking over the strange impression you gave me the first year. Eyes have always been terribly important to me in that I have imagined them to be the centre to be tapped upon for what may exist below. When I was able to meet your glance I had the eerie feeling that I had slipped an inscrutable vacancy. Rather as the archaic or sphinx-like. The probable answer to that was that I could only see my own state of mind reflected wherever I might look. This last year I felt the change in you and feel not only gladly shy but deeply grave about it. I have always supposed that evolution, after nature has adjusted the physical side to the best of her ability, lies within the individual. From the waking moment there is that attempt to balance mind matter and custom so that the life may utilize his time in space for more than the elementary perceptions. It is the keen adventure or imaginative pursuit that comes after the more tractable things are in leash.

LETTER TO BARONESS: The recipient of this letter and the nature of her relationship to Murray aren't clear. This sole extant draft ends incomplete.

PASSAGE ON READING: From the document archived as "The Hills and the Hollows," a blank-verse memoir Murray wrote about her childhood. Given the prose style of the passage, however, this untitled text is most likely separate from that document. GC included a version of the passage in *A Faun Surmising*.

Changed "Culmn" to "Colum." Changed "Guety" to "Goethe."

DRAFTS, FRAGMENTS, AND POEMS

Poems in this section have never appeared in any publication. The selection was made from Murray's original typed manuscripts, as well as from her numerous notebooks and letters.

STERILITY: Dated Monday, June 15, 1936.

SONG ("SOMEWHERE LIES A SILVER LAND"): Dated Thursday, June 11, 1936. Murray, on a few occasions, gave her own poems grades, according to her rubric of A=OK, B=So-So, C=Bad. This one was marked with the rare "A."

"NOW WHETHER THE DEAD ARE HERE?": From a letter dated August 2, 1939, written to her mother while on a trip through Vermont, and which GC included in *A Faun Surmising*.

THE DREAM OF THE ARCHITECT: "To the cults of contrition or imitation": "imitation" appears as "initation" and so another alternative could be "initiation."

"WOMAN WHOSE BODY": The original "panting" was kept considering her repeated use of this word in other poems; "planting" may have been intended or simply appears here as a ghost rhyme.

"BLACK PEOPLE, YOU LISTEN TO ME,": Parenthetical that starts the poem appears in a letter Murray wrote to her mother.

"WHEN MOONLIGHT SKIES ARE NEW": Dated August 7, 1936.

"IN THE EVENING OVER THE WELL CURVED HILLS": Changed "repation" to "repetition."

"YOU LIKE STARS BLESS!": Changed "Of a broken not" to "Of a broken knot."

VISION IN ARCAID: Dated July 28, 1938.

JINGLE: Dated Sunday, June 21, 1936.

FATA MORGANA: Another poem Murray graded "A." See note above for "Song."

SHEPHERD BOY'S LAMENT: Dated July 6, 1936.

"THE THROBBING SOB OF DANCE NIGHT THINGS,": Dated Sunday, June 21, 1936.

"PEARL LUSTRED": Dated August 12, 1936.

A TEAR: Dated June 1936.

"THEIR DAUGHTER IS THERE ALONE AS SHE MUST BE": GC included this stanza in "Instinct and Sleep" in *Poems* (1947). Nothing in the original manuscripts suggests that it is part of that poem.